United States Government Accountability Office

Report to the Chairman, Committee on Commerce, Science, and Transportation, U.S. Senate

I0448390

September 2013

INFORMATION RESELLERS

Consumer Privacy Framework Needs to Reflect Changes in Technology and the Marketplace

INFORMATION RESELLERS

Consumer Privacy Framework Needs to Reflect Changes in Technology and the Marketplace

GAO Highlights

Highlights of GAO-13-663, a report to the Chairman, Committee on Commerce, Science, and Transportation, U.S. Senate

Why GAO Did This Study

In recent years, information resellers—companies that collect and resell information on individuals—dramatically increased the collection and sharing of personal data for marketing purposes, raising privacy concerns among some in Congress. Recent growth in the use of social media, mobile applications, and other technologies intensified these concerns. GAO was asked to examine privacy issues and information resellers. This report addresses (1) privacy laws applicable to consumer information held by resellers, (2) gaps in the law that may exist, and (3) views on approaches for improving consumer data privacy.

To address these objectives, GAO analyzed laws, studies, and other documents, and interviewed representatives of federal agencies, the reseller and marketing industries, consumer and privacy groups, and others. GAO focused primarily on consumer information used for marketing purposes.

What GAO Recommends

Congress should consider strengthening the consumer privacy framework to reflect the effects of changes in technology and the increased market for consumer information. Any changes should seek to provide consumers with appropriate privacy protections without unduly inhibiting commerce and innovation. The Department of Commerce agreed that strengthened privacy protections could better protect consumers and support innovation.

View GAO-13-663. For more information, contact Alicia Puente Cackley at (202) 512-8678 or cackleya@gao.gov.

What GAO Found

No overarching federal privacy law governs the collection and sale of personal information among private-sector companies, including information resellers. Instead, a variety of laws tailored to specific purposes, situations, or entities governs the use, sharing, and protection of personal information. For example, the Fair Credit Reporting Act limits the use and distribution of personal information collected or used to help determine eligibility for such things as credit or employment, but does not apply to information used for marketing. Other laws apply specifically to health care providers, financial institutions, videotape service providers, or to the online collection of information about children.

The current statutory framework for consumer privacy does not fully address new technologies—such as the tracking of online behavior or mobile devices—and the vastly increased marketplace for personal information, including the proliferation of information sharing among third parties. With regard to data used for marketing, no federal statute provides consumers the right to learn what information is held about them and who holds it. In many circumstances, consumers also do not have the legal right to control the collection or sharing with third parties of sensitive personal information (such as their shopping habits and health interests) for marketing purposes. As a result, although some industry participants have stated that current privacy laws are adequate—particularly in light of self-regulatory measures under way—GAO found that gaps exist in the current statutory framework for privacy. And that the framework does not fully reflect the Fair Information Practice Principles, widely accepted principles for protecting the privacy and security of personal information that have served as a basis for many of the privacy recommendations federal agencies have made.

Views differ on the approach that any new privacy legislation or regulation should take. Some privacy advocates generally have argued that a comprehensive overarching privacy law would provide greater consistency and address gaps in law left by the current sector-specific approach. Other stakeholders have stated that a comprehensive, one-size-fits-all approach to privacy would be burdensome and inflexible. In addition, some privacy advocates have cited the need for legislation that would provide consumers with greater ability to access, control the use of, and correct information about them, particularly with respect to data used for purposes other than those for which they originally were provided. At the same time, industry representatives have asserted that restrictions on the collection and use of personal data would impose compliance costs, inhibit innovation and efficiency, and reduce consumer benefits, such as more relevant advertising and beneficial products and services. Nonetheless, the rapid increase in the amount and type of personal information that is collected and resold warrants reconsideration of how well the current privacy framework protects personal information. The challenge will be providing appropriate privacy protections without unduly inhibiting the benefits to consumers, commerce, and innovation that data sharing can accord.

Contents

Letter		1
	Background	2
	Several Laws Apply in Specific Circumstances to Consumer Data That Resellers Hold	7
	Existing Privacy Laws Have Limited Scope over Personal Data Used for Marketing	16
	Views Differ on Specific versus Comprehensive Approaches to Privacy Law and on Consumer Interests	31
	Conclusions	46
	Matter for Congressional Consideration	46
	Agency Comments	47

Appendix I	Objectives, Scope, and Methodology	48

Appendix II	Examples of Data Collected and Used by Information Resellers	52

Appendix III	Comments from the Department of Commerce	54

Appendix IV	GAO Contact and Staff Acknowledgments	56

Tables

Table 1: Fair Information Practice Principles	6
Table 2: Selected Examples of Consumer Data in Acxiom's Marketing Products, 2012	52
Table 3: Selected Examples of Marketing Lists Available from Experian, 2012	53

Figures

Figure 1: Typical Flow of Consumer Data through Resellers to Third-Party Users	3
Figure 2: Dates of Enactment of Key Federal Privacy Laws and the Introduction of New Technologies	21

Abbreviations

CFAA	Computer Fraud and Abuse Act
COPPA	Children's Online Privacy Protection Act
ECPA	Electronic Communications Privacy Act
EU	European Union
FCRA	Fair Credit Reporting Act
FIPPs	Fair Information Practice Principles
FTC	Federal Trade Commission
GLBA	Gramm-Leach-Bliley Act
HIPAA	Health Insurance Portability and Accountability Act
OECD	Organisation for Economic Co-operation and Development

GAO

441 G St. N.W.
Washington, DC 20548

U.S. GOVERNMENT ACCOUNTABILITY OFFICE

September 25, 2013

The Honorable John D. Rockefeller IV
Chairman
Committee on Commerce, Science, and Transportation
United States Senate

Dear Mr. Chairman:

Some members of Congress and others have raised privacy concerns about the collection and use of consumers' personal information by information resellers—companies with a primary line of business of collecting, aggregating, and selling personal information to third parties. In part, their concerns stem from consumers not always knowing the nature and extent of the information collected about them and how it is used and shared. The information reseller industry has grown significantly in recent years, as has the amount of consumer information that these companies assemble and distribute. Moreover, growing use of the Internet, social media, and mobile applications has intensified privacy concerns because these media greatly facilitate the ability to gather increasing amounts of personal information, track online behavior, and monitor locations and activities.

You asked us to review privacy issues related to consumer data collected, used, and shared by information resellers. This report examines (1) existing federal laws and regulations relating to the privacy of consumer information held by information resellers, (2) any gaps that may exist in this legal framework, and (3) views on approaches for improving consumer data privacy. This report focuses primarily on privacy issues related to consumer information used for marketing and for individual reference services (also known as look-up or people-search services); it does not focus on information used for other purposes, such as fraud prevention and eligibility for credit or employment.[1]

---

[1] In 2006, we issued a report examining financial institutions' use of information resellers, which focused largely on consumer information used to make eligibility determinations for credit, insurance, and employment, comply with certain legal requirements, and prevent fraud. GAO, *Personal Information: Key Federal Privacy Laws Do Not Require Information Resellers to Safeguard All Sensitive Data*, GAO-06-674 (Washington, D.C.: June 26, 2006).

To address the first and second objectives, we reviewed and analyzed relevant federal laws, regulations, and enforcement actions, and selected state laws. We interviewed representatives of federal agencies, trade associations, consumer and privacy groups, and information resellers to obtain their views on federal data privacy laws related to information resellers, including the adequacy of consumers' ability to access, correct, opt out, or request deletion of information. To address the third objective, we identified and reviewed approaches for improving consumer data privacy through legislative, regulatory, or self-regulatory means that federal entities—including the White House, Federal Trade Commission (FTC), and Department of Commerce (Commerce)—or representatives of industry, consumer, and privacy groups have advocated. We also interviewed representatives of these entities and reviewed relevant studies, congressional hearing records, position papers, public comments, and other sources. Appendix I contains a more extensive discussion of our scope and methodology.

We conducted this performance audit from August 2012 through September 2013, in accordance with generally accepted government auditing standards. Those standards require that we plan and perform the audit to obtain sufficient, appropriate evidence to provide a reasonable basis for our findings and conclusions based on our audit objectives. We believe that the evidence obtained provides a reasonable basis for our findings and conclusions based on our audit objectives.

Background

Information resellers—sometimes also called data brokers, data aggregators, or information solutions providers—offer several types of products to customers that include retailers, advertisers, private individuals, nonprofit organizations, and law enforcement and other government agencies. Consumer reporting agencies—including the three nationwide credit bureaus, Equifax, Experian, and TransUnion—provide consumer reports that commonly are used to determine eligibility for credit, employment, and insurance. Some resellers offer products that help companies comply with legal requirements or identify, investigate, and prevent fraudulent transactions (for example, by enabling confirmation of a customer's identity). Some information resellers, such as Spokeo and Intelius, also offer individual reference services that sell personal identifying information about consumers to individuals or companies.

In addition, many information resellers, such as Acxiom and LexisNexis, offer products that companies use for marketing purposes. Resellers may focus on groups of likely customers who share common characteristics, and therefore may have similar interests or preferences. For example, resellers may offer information products that allow clients to target their online advertisements and help ensure that promotional materials are sent to the most relevant individuals. Resellers may offer retailers the ability to add purchase and lifestyle information to their existing customer databases. In addition, resellers may offer clients marketing lists with contact information of prospective customers.

Resellers maintain large, sophisticated databases with information from a variety of sources about individuals and families. The consumer information that each reseller maintains and sells varies, but can include names, addresses, family members, neighbors, credit histories, motor vehicle records, insurance claims, criminal records, employment histories, incomes, ethnicities, purchase histories, interests, and hobbies. (See appendix II for a detailed list of examples of the types of consumer information held by information resellers.) As shown in figure 1, resellers obtain their information from three primary types of sources: public records, publicly available information, and nonpublic information.

Figure 1: Typical Flow of Consumer Data through Resellers to Third-Party Users

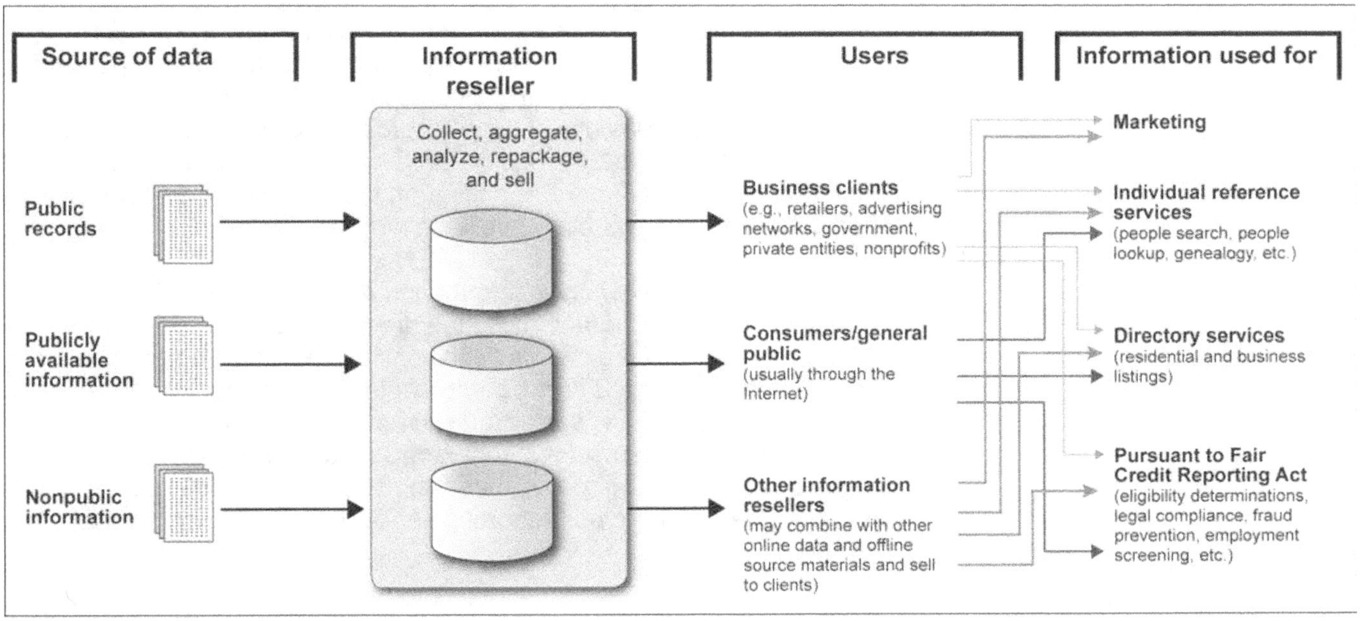

Source: GAO.

GAO-13-663 Information Resellers

- *Public records*, available to anyone, generally are obtained from governmental entities. What constitutes a public record depends on state and federal laws, but may include birth and death records, property records, tax lien and assessor files, voter registrations, licensing records, and court records (including criminal records, bankruptcy filings, civil case files, and legal judgments).

- *Publicly available information* is not found in public records, but nevertheless is publicly available through sources such as telephone directories, business directories, classified advertisements, newspapers or magazines, and other materials.

- *Nonpublic information* derives from proprietary sources. For example, consumers may provide the information directly to businesses through loyalty card programs at grocery or retail stores, website registrations, warranty registrations, contests, surveys and questionnaires, and purchase histories. Resellers (or a third party such as a website operator acting on behalf of the reseller) also may collect nonpublic information about consumers' online locations and actions, including a computer's Internet protocol address, the browser used, activities during a consumer's visit to a website (such as search terms or purchases), and activities conducted on other websites.

Consumer information can be derived from mobile networks, devices (including smartphones and tablets), operating systems, and applications. In addition, resellers may obtain personal information from the profile or public information areas of websites, including social media sites such as Facebook, LinkedIn, MySpace, and Twitter, or from information posted to blogs or discussion forums. Depending on the context, information from these sources may be publicly available or nonpublic.

There is limited publicly known information about the information reseller industry as a whole. Characterizing the precise size and nature of the industry can be difficult because definitions for resellers vary and data on resellers often are limited or not comparable. For example, the U.S. Census Bureau (Census) does not assign a business classification code specific to information resellers. Instead, Census has assigned different primary codes, including "data processing and preparation," "direct mail advertising services," "credit reporting services," and "information retrieval services."[2] Thus, Census data cannot be used to provide a reliable count or other statistical information on the information resellers industry as a whole. According to FTC and Commerce, there is no comprehensive list or registry of companies that resell personal information. Several privacy-related organizations and websites maintain lists of information resellers—for example, Privacy Rights Clearinghouse lists more than 250 on its website—but none of these lists claim to be comprehensive. The Direct Marketing Association, which represents companies and nonprofits that use and support data-driven marketing, maintains a proprietary membership list, which it says numbers about 2,500 organizations (although that includes retailers and others that typically would not be considered information resellers).

FTC has called on the information reseller industry to improve the transparency of its practices, and in December 2012 issued orders requiring nine information resellers to provide FTC with information about how they collect and use data about consumers.[3] FTC sought details about the nature and sources of the consumer information that information resellers collect; how they use, maintain, and disseminate the information; and the extent to which the companies allow consumers to access and correct their information or opt out of having their personal information sold. According to FTC staff, the agency expects to issue a report with findings by the end of 2013.

The Fair Information Practice Principles (FIPPs) are a set of internationally recognized principles for protecting the privacy and security of personal information. A U.S. government advisory committee first proposed the practices in 1973 in response to concerns about the consequences computerized data systems could have on the privacy of personal information. While the FIPPs are principles as opposed to legal requirements, they provide a framework for balancing the need for privacy with other interests. The Organisation for Economic Co-operation and

---

[2]Census assigns business classification codes, including Standard Industrial Classification and North American Classification System codes, to each company to classify its main industry and line of business.

[3]Federal Trade Commission, *Order to File Special Report*, File No. P125404 (Dec. 14, 2012). The order was pursuant to the agency's *Resolution Directing Use of the Compulsory Process to Collect Information Regarding Data Brokers*, File No. P125404 (Dec. 14, 2012). The nine companies were Acxiom, CoreLogic, Datalogix, eBureau, ID Analytics, Intelius, PeekYou, Rapleaf, and Recorded Future.

Development (OECD) developed a revised version of the FIPPs in 1980 that has been widely adopted (see table 1).[4]

Table 1: Fair Information Practice Principles

Principle	Description
Collection limitation	The collection of personal information should be limited, obtained by lawful and fair means, and, where appropriate, with the knowledge or consent of the individual.
Data quality	Personal information should be relevant to the purpose for which it is collected, and should be accurate, complete, and current as needed for that purpose.
Purpose specification	The purposes for the collection of personal information should be disclosed before collection and upon any change to those purposes, and the use of the information should be limited to those purposes and compatible purposes.
Use limitation	Personal information should not be disclosed or otherwise used for other than a specified purpose without consent of the individual or legal authority.
Security safeguards	Personal information should be protected with reasonable security safeguards against risks such as loss or unauthorized access, destruction, use, modification, or disclosure.
Openness	The public should be informed about privacy policies and practices, and individuals should have ready means of learning about the use of personal information.
Individual participation	Individuals should have the following rights: to know about the collection of personal information, to access that information, to request correction, and to challenge the denial of those rights.
Accountability	Individuals controlling the collection or use of personal information should be accountable for taking steps to ensure the implementation of these principles.

Source: OECD.

Many organizations and governments have used these principles, with some variation, as best practices. In the United States, the FIPPs served as the basis for the Privacy Act—which governs the collection, maintenance, use, and dissemination of personal information by federal agencies—and as the basis for many of the privacy recommendations of agencies such as FTC and Commerce. The FIPPs also served as the basis for a framework for consumer data privacy that the White House issued in February 2012. This framework presents a consumer privacy bill

---

[4]Organisation for Economic Co-operation and Development, *Guidelines on the Protection of Privacy and Transborder Flow of Personal Data* (Paris, France: Sept. 23, 1980). OECD produces internationally agreed-upon instruments, decisions, and recommendations to promote rules in areas where multilateral agreement is necessary for individual countries to make progress in the global economy. Its 30 member countries include the United States. OECD has been reviewing whether its privacy guidelines should be revised or updated to take into account the change in the role of personal data in the economy and society.

of rights, describes a stakeholder process to specify how the principles in that bill of rights would apply, and encourages Congress to provide FTC with enforcement authorities for the bill of rights.[5]

Several Laws Apply in Specific Circumstances to Consumer Data That Resellers Hold

Currently, no comprehensive federal privacy law governs the collection, use, and sale of personal information by private-sector companies. There are also no federal laws designed specifically to address all the products sold and information maintained by information resellers. In contrast, a baseline privacy law exists for personal information the federal government maintains—the Privacy Act of 1974.[6] The act, among other things, generally prohibits, subject to a number of exceptions, the disclosure by federal entities of records about an individual without the individual's written consent and provides U.S. persons with a means to seek access to and amend their records.[7] Many other industrialized countries have implemented baseline privacy laws for information held by private-sector companies. The 28 member countries of the European Union have implemented into their national laws the union's 1995 Data Protection Directive, which provides a comprehensive framework on the protection of personal data.[8] It states that the personal information of European Union citizens may not be transmitted to nations outside of the union unless those countries are deemed to have "adequate" data protection laws.

Primary Federal Privacy Laws

In the United States, the federal privacy framework for private-sector companies comprises a set of more narrowly tailored laws that govern the use and protection of personal information—that is, the laws apply for specific purposes, in certain situations, to certain sectors, or to certain types of entities. The primary federal laws with regard to consumer privacy include the following:

---

[5]The White House, *Consumer Data Privacy in a Networked World: A Framework for Protecting Privacy and Promoting Innovation in the Global Digital Economy* (Washington, D.C.: Feb. 23, 2012).

[6]Pub. L. No. 93-579, 88 Stat. 1896 (1974) (codified as amended at 5 U.S.C. § 552a).

[7]5 U.S.C. § 552a.

[8]European Union, *Directive 95/46/EC of the European Parliament and of the Council on the Protection of Individuals with Regard to the Processing of Personal Data and the Free Movement of Such Data* (Oct. 24, 1995).

Fair Credit Reporting Act (FCRA).[9] Enacted in 1970, FCRA protects the security and confidentiality of personal information collected or used to help make decisions about individuals' eligibility for such products as credit or for insurance or employment.[10] FCRA applies to "consumer reporting agencies" that provide "consumer reports" that contain credit histories and other personal information and are used for eligibility determinations.[11] Accordingly, FCRA applies to the three nationwide consumer reporting agencies (commonly called credit bureaus) and to any other information resellers that resell consumer reports for use by others. FCRA limits resellers' use and distribution of personal data—for example, by allowing consumers to opt out of allowing consumer reporting agencies to share their personal information with third parties for prescreened marketing offers. The act also allows individuals to access and dispute the accuracy of personal data held on them. Additionally, as amended in 2003, FCRA imposes safeguarding requirements designed to prevent identity theft and assist identity theft victims.[12]

Gramm-Leach-Bliley Act (GLBA).[13] Enacted in 1999, GLBA protects nonpublic personal information that individuals provide to financial

---

[9]Pub. L. No. 91-508, Tit. VI, 84 Stat. 1114, 1128 (1970) (codified as amended at 15 U.S.C. §§ 1681-1681x).

[10]*See* 15 U.S.C. § 1681.

[11]FCRA defines a consumer reporting agency as "any person which, for monetary fees, dues, or on a cooperative nonprofit basis, regularly engages in whole or in part in the practice of assembling or evaluating consumer credit information or other information on consumers for the purpose of furnishing consumer reports to third parties, and which uses any means or facility of interstate commerce for the purpose of preparing or furnishing consumer reports." 15 U.S.C. § 1681a(f). The act defines consumer report as "any written, oral, or other communication of any information by a consumer reporting agency bearing on a consumer's credit worthiness, credit standing, credit capacity, character, general reputation, personal characteristics, or mode of living which is used or expected to be used or collected in whole or in part for the purpose of serving as a factor in establishing the consumer's eligibility for (A) credit or insurance to be used primarily for personal, family, or household purposes; (B) employment purposes; or (C) any other purpose authorized under section 604 [of the FCRA]," subject to certain exclusions. 15 U.S.C. § 1681a(d).

[12]Fair and Accurate Credit Transactions Act of 2003, Pub. L. No. 108-159, 117 Stat. 1952 (2003).

[13]Pub. L. No. 106-102, 113 Stat. 1338 (1999) (codified as amended in scattered sections of 12 and 15 U.S.C.).

institutions or that such institutions maintain.[14] GLBA sharing and disclosure restrictions apply to entities that fall under GLBA's definition of a "financial institution" or that receive nonpublic personal information from such a financial institution.[15] The act's privacy provisions restrict the sharing of nonpublic personal information collected by or acquired from financial institutions, which include those resellers covered by GLBA's definition of financial institution. Under a "reuse and redisclosure" provision, a nonaffiliated third party that receives nonpublic personal information from a financial institution faces restrictions on how it may further share or use the information.[16] For example, a third party that receives nonpublic personal information from a financial institution to process consumers' account transactions may not use the information for its marketing purposes or sell it to another entity for marketing purposes. GLBA requires financial regulators to establish appropriate standards for financial institutions relating to administrative, technical, and physical safeguards to ensure the security and confidentiality of customer records and information; protect against any anticipated threats or hazards to the security or integrity of such records; and protect against unauthorized access to or use of such records or information that could result in substantial harm or inconvenience to any customer.[17]

Health Insurance Portability and Accountability Act (HIPAA).[18] Enacted in 1996, HIPAA establishes a set of national standards for the protection of certain health information. The HIPAA privacy rule governs the use and disclosure of an individual's health information for purposes

---

[14]*See* 15 U.S.C. §§ 6801-6802. Subtitle A of Title V of the act contains the privacy provisions relating to the disclosure of nonpublic personal information. 15 U.S.C. §§ 6801-6809.

[15]15 U.S.C. § 6802. GLBA defines a "financial institution" as any institution the business of which is engaging in financial activities as described in section 4(k) of the Bank Holding Company Act (12 U.S.C. § 1843(k)). 15 U.S.C. § 6809(3)(a). Such activities include lending, providing financial or investment advice, and insuring against loss.

[16]15 U.S.C. § 6802(c).

[17]15 U.S.C. § 6801. For example, the FTC safeguards rule implements GLBA's requirements for entities that fall under FTC jurisdiction, including check-cashing businesses, payday lenders, and mortgage brokers. *See* 15 C.F.R. Part 314.

[18]Pub. L. No. 104-191, 110 Stat. 1936 (1996) (codified as amended in scattered sections of 18, 26, 29, and 42 U.S.C.).

including marketing.[19] According to guidance from the Department of Health and Human Services, the rule aims to strike a balance that permits important uses of information in the provision of health care while protecting patients' privacy.[20] With some exceptions, the rule requires an individual's written authorization before a covered entity—a health care provider that transmits health information electronically in connection with covered transactions, health care clearinghouse, or health plan—may use or disclose that individual's protected health information for marketing.[21] In addition, HIPAA requires covered entities to safeguard protected personal health information and protect against any reasonably anticipated unauthorized uses or disclosures of such information, among other things.[22] The act does not directly restrict the use, disclosure, or resale of protected health information by information resellers or other parties not considered HIPAA-covered entities.

Children's Online Privacy Protection Act (COPPA).[23] Enacted in 1998, COPPA governs the online collection of personal information from children under 13 by operators of websites or online services, including mobile applications.[24] Specifically, COPPA and its implementing regulations apply to the collection of personal information—such as full name, e-mail address, or geolocation information—that would allow someone to identify or contact a child. The law requires covered website and online service operators to obtain verifiable parental consent before collecting such information. It also specifies what information must be included in the notice provided to parents and how and when to acquire

---

[19]45 C.F.R. Parts 160, 164.

[20]Department of Health and Human Services, "Summary of HIPAA Privacy Provisions," last revised May 2003, available at http://hhs.gov/ocr/privacy/hipaa/understanding/summary/.

[21]The HIPAA privacy rule carves out specific exceptions to its definition of "marketing" that include communications regarding refill reminders, communications to individuals from a covered entity's benefit plan that describe health-related products or services provided by or included in a benefit plan, communications about participating providers in a provider or health plan network, communications for treatment of individuals, and communications for case management or care coordination for an individual. 45 C.F.R. § 164.501.

[22]42 U.S.C. § 1320d-2(d)(2); *see also* 45 C.F.R. Part 164, Subpart C.

[23]Pub. L. No. 105-277, Div. C, Tit. XIII, 112 Stat. 2681-728 (1998) (codified at 15 U.S.C. §§ 6501-6506).

[24]FTC issued regulations implementing COPPA, 16 C.F.R. Part 312.

parental consent. Although COPPA may not directly affect information resellers, COPPA governs information collection by operators of websites and online services, both of which are potential sources of personal information for resellers and other parties. COPPA would not apply to the collection of a child's information from the child's parent or other adults.

Electronic Communications Privacy Act (ECPA).[25] Among its provisions, ECPA, which was enacted in 1986, prohibits the interception and disclosure of electronic communications by third parties unless an exception applies, such as one of the parties to the communication having consented to the interception or disclosure.[26] For example, the act would prevent an Internet service provider from selling the content of its customers' e-mails and text messages to an information reseller that wanted to use the content for marketing purposes unless the customers had given their consent for the disclosures. However, ECPA provides more limited protection for information that is considered to be "non-content", such as a customer's name and address.[27]

Federal Trade Commission Act (FTC Act), Section 5.[28] Enacted in 1914, the FTC Act prohibits unfair or deceptive acts or practices in or affecting commerce. Although the act does not explicitly grant FTC the specific authority to protect privacy, it has been interpreted to apply to deceptions or violations of written privacy policies. For example, if a retailer had a written privacy policy stating it would not share customers' personal information with resellers or other third parties for any purposes and later breached the policy by selling the information to such parties, FTC could prosecute the retailer for unfair and deceptive practices. Likewise, the act would apply to resellers if they used personal information for purposes prohibited by their written privacy policies. In

---

[25]Pub. L. No. 99-508, 100 Stat. 1848 (1986) (codified as amended in scattered sections of 18 U.S.C.).

[26]*See* 18 U.S.C. §§ 2701-2712.

[27]18 U.S.C. § 2703(c)(2), cited by U.S. Department of Justice, Computer Crime and Intellectual Property Section, *Searching and Seizing Computers and Obtaining Electronic Evidence in Criminal Investigations*, Chapter 3 (2009), available at http://justice.gov/criminal/cybercrime/docs/ssmanual2009.pdf.

[28]15 U.S.C. § 45. Section 5 of the FTC Act, as originally enacted, only related to "unfair methods of competition." The Wheeler-Lea Act, passed in 1938, expanded the Commission's jurisdiction to include "unfair or deceptive acts or practices." Wheeler-Lea Amendments of 1938, Pub. L. No. 75-447, 52 Stat. 111.

addition, the FTC Act's unfairness authority could apply, even in the absence of a privacy policy, in situations involving a likelihood of substantial injury to consumers that is not reasonably avoidable and not offset by countervailing benefits. In effect, FTC enforcement actions can establish compliance requirements that companies can follow in order to avoid future enforcement actions.[29]

Selected Additional Applicable Laws

As they relate to specific types of consumer services or types of records, other federal privacy laws that also may apply to information resellers' practices and products include the following:[30]

Driver's Privacy Protection Act.[31] Enacted in 1994, the act generally prohibits the use and disclosure of certain personal information in state motor vehicle records.[32] The act also specifies permissible uses of personal information, and that an authorized recipient of personal information may "resell or redisclose" the information only for purposes permitted by law.[33] For example, a state department of motor vehicles cannot sell drivers' personal information to resellers for marketing purposes unless the department obtained consent from the individuals.[34]

---

[29]FTC has also required implementation of a comprehensive privacy policy as part of the settlement of FTC charges. *See In the Matter of Google Inc.,* FTC File No. 102 3136, decision and order (Oct. 13, 2011).

[30]While these are some relevant examples of subject-specific privacy laws, this is not a comprehensive list of all federal privacy laws that could apply to information resellers.

[31]Pub. L. No. 103-322, Tit. XXX, 108 Stat. 2099 (1994) (codified as amended at 18 U.S.C. §§ 2721-2725).

[32]*See* 18 U.S.C. § 2721.

[33]Permissible uses include use by a government agency in carrying out its functions and uses related to matters of motor vehicle or driver safety and theft. *See* 18 U.S.C. § 2721(b) for a complete listing of permissible uses.

[34] In July 2013, the Court of Appeals for the Second Circuit determined that data brokers could be liable for the use of personal information that they obtain from state departments of motor vehicles and sell to others. The court held that the Driver's Privacy Protection Act imposes a duty on resellers to exercise reasonable care in responding to requests for personal information drawn from motor vehicle records. *Gordon v. Softech, Int'l, Inc.,* No. 12-661-cv. 2013 WL 3939442, at *12 (2d Cir. July 31, 2013).

Family Educational Rights and Privacy Act.[35] Enacted in 1974, the act governs access to and disclosure of students' education records to parents, students, and third parties. Specifically, the act provides that no federal funds shall be made available to any school or institution that has a policy of releasing students' education records or personally identifiable information contained in such records (other than directory information) to third parties such as information resellers (other than to certain parties and for certain purposes enumerated in the statute) without written consent from the students' parents.[36, 37]

Video Privacy Protection Act.[38] Enacted in 1988, the act prohibits a video tape service provider from knowingly disclosing personally identifiable information concerning video rental and sales records, including the title or subject matter of any video tapes, to third parties, subject to exceptions.[39] However, a provider may disclose the names and addresses of consumers to third parties if the consumer has had the opportunity to prohibit such disclosure. The provider also may disclose the content of rental materials if that information will be used only to market goods and services directly to the consumer.

Computer Fraud and Abuse Act (CFAA).[40] Enacted in 1986, CFAA makes the knowing unauthorized access of computers a crime. CFAA is not specifically a privacy law but can serve to restrict a third party from

---

[35]Pub. L. No. 93-380, Tit. V, § 513, 88 Stat. 57 (1974) (codified as amended at 20 U.S.C. § 1232g).

[36]20 U.S.C. § 1232g(b)(1). A student may provide consent to release education records and personal information if he or she is 18 years of age or older or is attending a postsecondary education institution. For students younger than 18, consent of their parents is necessary. *See* 20 U.S.C. § 1232g(d).

[37]For the purposes of this section, the term "directory information" relating to a student includes the following: the student's name, address, telephone listing, date and place of birth, major field of study, participation in officially recognized activities and sports, weight and height of members of athletic teams, dates of attendance, degrees and awards received, and the most recent previous educational agency or institution attended by the student. *See* 20 U.S.C. § 1232g(a)(5)(A).

[38]Pub. L. No. 100-618, 102 Stat. 3195 (1988) (codified as amended at 18 U.S.C. § 2710).

[39]18 U.S.C. § 2710.

[40]Pub. L. No. 99-474, 100 Stat. 1213 (1986) (codified as amended at 18 U.S.C. § 1030).

collecting personal information from a website when the collection would violate the site's terms of service.[41]

Telecommunications Act.[42] Enacted in 1996, the act requires telecommunications carriers to protect the confidentiality of proprietary information of customers.[43] Additionally, the act prohibits carriers from using proprietary information from other carriers for their own marketing efforts.

Selected State Privacy Laws

While we did not conduct a comprehensive review of all state laws, we identified relatively few state laws that broadly address consumer privacy rights or regulate information resellers. Representatives of several privacy advocacy organizations similarly noted that few state laws broadly address information resellers or consumer privacy, such as the collection or disclosure of personal information held by private companies. However, some states have enacted laws designed to improve data security and reduce identity theft, such as laws requiring consumer notification of security breaches involving personal information.[44]

In addition, we reviewed the laws of four states that impose disclosure requirements related to the sharing of personal information about

---

[41]Courts have held that CFAA prohibits access to websites when that access exceeds the sites' terms of use or end-user license agreements. *See, e.g., Snap-On Bus. Solutions Inc. v. O'Neil & Assoc., Inc.*, 708 F.Supp. 2d 669 (N.D. Ohio 2010); *Southwest Airlines Co. v. Farechase, Inc.*, 318 F.Supp. 2d 435 (N.D. Tex. 2004); *America Online, Inc. v. LCGM, Inc.*, 46 F.Supp. 2d 444 (E.D. Va. 1998).

[42]Pub. L. No. 104-104, 110 Stat. 56 (1996) (codified as amended in scattered sections of 15 and 47 U.S.C.).

[43]47 U.S.C. § 222(a).

[44]According to the National Conference of State Legislatures, as of August 2012, 46 states, the District of Columbia, Guam, Puerto Rico, and the Virgin Islands had enacted legislation requiring data-breach notifications. In general, these states and territories require companies to notify state or territorial residents if their personal information in the companies' custody was compromised. See National Conference of State Legislatures: *State Security Breach Notification Laws*, available at http://www.ncsl.org/issues-research/telecom/security-breach-notification-laws.aspx.

consumers.[45] California's Shine the Light law requires certain businesses to disclose, upon a California customer's request, whether those businesses have shared the customer's personal information with third parties for direct marketing purposes.[46] For certain specified categories of information, the business also must notify the requesting consumer of the categories of information shared with a third party.[47] Similarly, Utah's Notice of Intent to Sell Nonpublic Personal Information Act requires commercial entities to disclose to consumers the types of nonpublic personal information shared with or sold to third parties for compensation.[48] Massachusetts and Nevada have laws or regulations requiring businesses to safeguard and encrypt personally identifiable consumer data. The Massachusetts regulations establish minimum standards for safeguarding personal information in both paper and electronic records and cover only personal information about residents of Massachusetts.[49] The Nevada law generally covers any personal information belonging to certain categories that a business maintains.[50]

---

[45]In 2011, the Supreme Court determined that a Vermont law that restricted the sale, disclosure, and use of pharmacy records that reveal the prescribing practices of individual doctors violated the First Amendment. The Vermont law provided that the prescriber-identifying information could not be sold by pharmacies for marketing purposes or used for marketing by pharmaceutical manufacturers. Pharmacies could share the information with anyone for any purpose except marketing. The Court determined that these content-and-speaker-based restrictions on speech were subject to heightened judicial scrutiny. Vermont's asserted interest in physician confidentiality did not withstand the heightened scrutiny. *Sorrell v. IMS Health, Inc,* 131 S.Ct. 2653 (2011).

[46]Cal. Civ. Code § 1798.83 (West). Any California resident with whom a business has an established business relationship is entitled to disclosure of the business's information-sharing practices. The law applies to many businesses, but those with fewer than 20 employees and certain financial institutions that are in compliance with separate privacy requirements are exempt.

[47]These categories include, among other things, the customer's height, race, religion, telephone number, number of children, medical condition, Social Security number, bank account number, and credit card balance. Cal. Civ. Code § 1798.83(e)(6).

[48]Utah Code Ann. §§ 13-37-101 to -203 (West).

[49]201 Mass. Code Regs. 17.01 to 17.05.

[50]Nev. Rev. Stat. §§ 603A.010 to .920. The encryption and security measure requirements do not apply to data transmitted over a secure, private communication channel for approving or processing negotiable instruments, electronic fund transfers, or similar methods.

Existing Privacy Laws Have Limited Scope over Personal Data Used for Marketing

For consumer data used for marketing purposes, the privacy protections provided under federal law have been limited. Although the FIPPs call for restraint in the collection and use of personal information, the scope of protections provided under current law has been narrow in relation to (1) individuals' ability to access, control, and correct their personal data; (2) collection methods and sources and types of consumer information collected; and (3) new technologies, such as tracking of web activity and the use of mobile devices. However, views differ on whether privacy protections should be expanded and if this could best be done through legislation or self-regulation.

Laws Provide Individuals Limited Ability to Access, Control, and Correct Their Personal Data

Current federal privacy laws generally do not provide individuals the universal right to access, control, or correct personal information that resellers and private-sector companies use for marketing purposes. The "collection limitation" and "openness" principles of the FIPPs state that individuals should be able to know about and consent to the collection of their personal information, while the "individual participation" principle states they should have the right to access that information, request correction, and challenge the denial of those rights. However, none of the federal statutes that we examined generally requires information resellers to allow individuals to review their personal information in the resellers' possession intended for marketing or information retrieval purposes, control its use, or correct it.

Access rights

In relation to data used for marketing purposes, no federal statute provides consumers the right to learn what information is held about them and who holds it. As noted earlier, FCRA provides individuals with rights to access information from consumer reports used for eligibility determinations, but does not apply to personal information used for marketing (other than prescreened marketing offers). For example, an information reseller we interviewed said the company generally does not offer consumers the ability to see the personal information held about them for purposes not covered under FCRA. Additionally, in 2006 some resellers told us that they gave individuals opportunities to order summary reports that disclosed personal information maintained for non-FCRA purposes, but the extent of the information provided varied.[51]

---

[51]GAO-06-674.

Control rights	Consumers have limited legal rights to control what personal information is collected, maintained, used, and shared and how. Under FCRA, individuals can request that personal information not be shared with third parties for marketing unsolicited prescreened credit or insurance offers. GLBA's privacy provisions generally limit financial institutions from sharing nonpublic personal information with nonaffiliated third parties without first providing certain notice and, in some cases, opt-out rights to customers and other consumers. However, apart from these two cases, individuals do not have a right to require that their personal information not be collected, used, and shared for marketing purposes. Some trade associations, information resellers, and other companies voluntarily have developed opt-out mechanisms through which consumers can request that their personal information be excluded from resellers' marketing databases.[52] The Digital Advertising Alliance also has a program that calls for its members to provide consumer control over what data are collected and used for online behavioral or interest-based advertising.[53]
Correction rights	No federal law that we examined provides correction rights for information used for marketing or look-up purposes. Correction refers to consumers' ability to have resellers and other parties correct or delete inaccurate, incomplete, or unverifiable information. For information covered under FCRA, consumers have the right to dispute information held by resellers that is incomplete or inaccurate, have a claim investigated, and have any errors deleted or corrected. However, neither FCRA nor any other federal

---

[52]For example, on September 4, 2013, Acxiom unveiled an online consumer site (AboutTheData.com) that, according to Acxiom, will allow consumers to view and edit the data about them that Acxiom clients use for digital marketing. Additionally, the site will give consumers the ability to opt-out, or exclude their personal information from Acxiom's marketing database, according to the company.

[53]In online behavioral advertising, information about a consumer's computer browser habits helps build a profile about the computer user that can be used to target the specific web-based advertisements shown to that computer user. Advertising and marketing trade associations formed the nonprofit Digital Advertising Alliance in 2008 to develop and administer principles for online data collection and use. In October 2010, the industry created a self-regulatory program that was based on its *Self-Regulatory Principles for Online Behavioral Advertising* (issued in 2009). The program calls on member companies engaging in online behavioral advertising to provide (1) transparency about data collection; (2) consumer control over whether data are collected and used; (3) security for and limited retention of data collected and used; (4) consent to changes in an entity's data collection and use policies; and (5) limitations on the collection of specified categories of sensitive data for online behavioral advertising purposes.

law that we examined provides similar correction rights for information used for marketing or look-up purposes.

Laws Largely Do Not Address Data Collection Methods, Sources, and Types

The "data quality" and "purpose specification" principles of the FIPPs state that personal information should be relevant and limited to the purpose for which it was collected, and the "collection limitation" principle calls for confining the collection of personal information. However, the scope of current federal privacy laws is limited in addressing the methods by which, or the sources from which, information resellers and private-sector companies collect and aggregate personal information, or the types of information that may be collected for marketing or look-up purposes.

Methods for collecting personal data

Federal laws generally do not govern the methods resellers may use to collect personal information for marketing or look-up purposes. Examples of such methods include "web scraping"—sometimes called data extraction or web data mining—in which resellers, advertisers, and other parties use software to search the web for information about an individual or individuals, and extract and download bulk information from a particular website that contains consumer information. The marketing material of one company we reviewed advertised that for a fee it would provide information on any individual by extracting data and photographs from social media websites, blogs, or telephone and professional directory sites that contain e-mail addresses and other contact information. A website's terms-of-use may legally restrict such practices or password protections may help prevent them. Resellers or retailers also may collect personal information through indirect means. For example, some retailers ask consumers to provide their zip code when using a credit card at the time of purchase. The zip code can be combined with the name on the credit card to determine the consumer's address, telephone number, or other personal information that may be held in a marketing database.

Sources of personal data

Current law generally allows resellers to collect personal information from sources that include warranty registration cards, consumer surveys, and retailers, and online sources such as discussion boards, social media sites, blogs, web browsing histories, and searches. Current law does not require disclosure to consumers when their information is collected from these sources, including when consumers are unaware that the information will be used for marketing purposes.

Types of information collected	The federal laws that address the types of consumer information that can be collected and shared for marketing and look-up purposes have limited reach and application. Under most circumstances, information that many people may consider very personal or sensitive legally can be collected, shared, and used for marketing purposes. This can include information about an individual's physical and mental health, income and assets, mobile telephone numbers, shopping habits, personal interests, political affiliations, and sexual habits and orientation. For example, in 2009 testimony before Congress, a representative of the World Privacy Forum said that some marketers maintain lists that contain information on individuals' medical conditions, including mental health conditions.[54] HIPAA provisions apply only to covered entities and not, for example, to health-related marketing lists used by e-health websites or other noncovered entities. Information resellers that do not qualify as covered entities can collect and use information about consumers' health histories and treatments for marketing purposes. Although federal laws generally do not restrict the types of information resellers can collect and share for marketing, many companies voluntarily follow guidelines that recognize that sensitive personal information merits different treatment. For example, industry principles for online behavioral advertising call for consent from individuals for the collection of certain sensitive personal information—including financial account numbers, pharmaceutical prescriptions, and medical records.[55]

Current Law Does Not Directly Address Some Privacy Issues Raised by New Technology

The current privacy framework does not fully address new technologies. Developments such as social media, web tracking technologies, and mobile devices have enabled even cheaper, faster, and more detailed data collection and sharing among resellers and private-sector companies. In a 2013 report, FTC staff noted that the rapid growth of mobile technologies provided substantial benefits to both businesses and consumers, but also presented unique privacy challenges because

---

[54]House Committee on Energy and Commerce, Subcommittee on Communications, Technology, and the Internet, and Subcommittee on Commerce, Trade, and Consumer Protection, *Exploring the Offline and Online Collection and Use of Consumer Information*, 111th Cong., 1st sess., Nov. 19, 2009; see testimony of Pam Dixon, Executive Director, World Privacy Forum.

[55]Digital Advertising Alliance, *Self-Regulatory Principles Overview, Principles for Online Behavioral Advertising*, available at http://aboutads.info/obaprinciples. For personal information of children, the principles purport to apply the protective measures in COPPA.

mobile devices generally were personal to an individual, almost always on, could facilitate large amounts of data collection and sharing among many entities, and could identify a user's geographical location.[56] As shown in figure 2, the original enactment of several federal privacy laws predate these trends and technologies.

[56]Federal Trade Commission, *Mobile Privacy Disclosures: Building Trust through Transparency* (Washington, D.C.: February 2013).

Figure 2: Dates of Enactment of Key Federal Privacy Laws and the Introduction of New Technologies

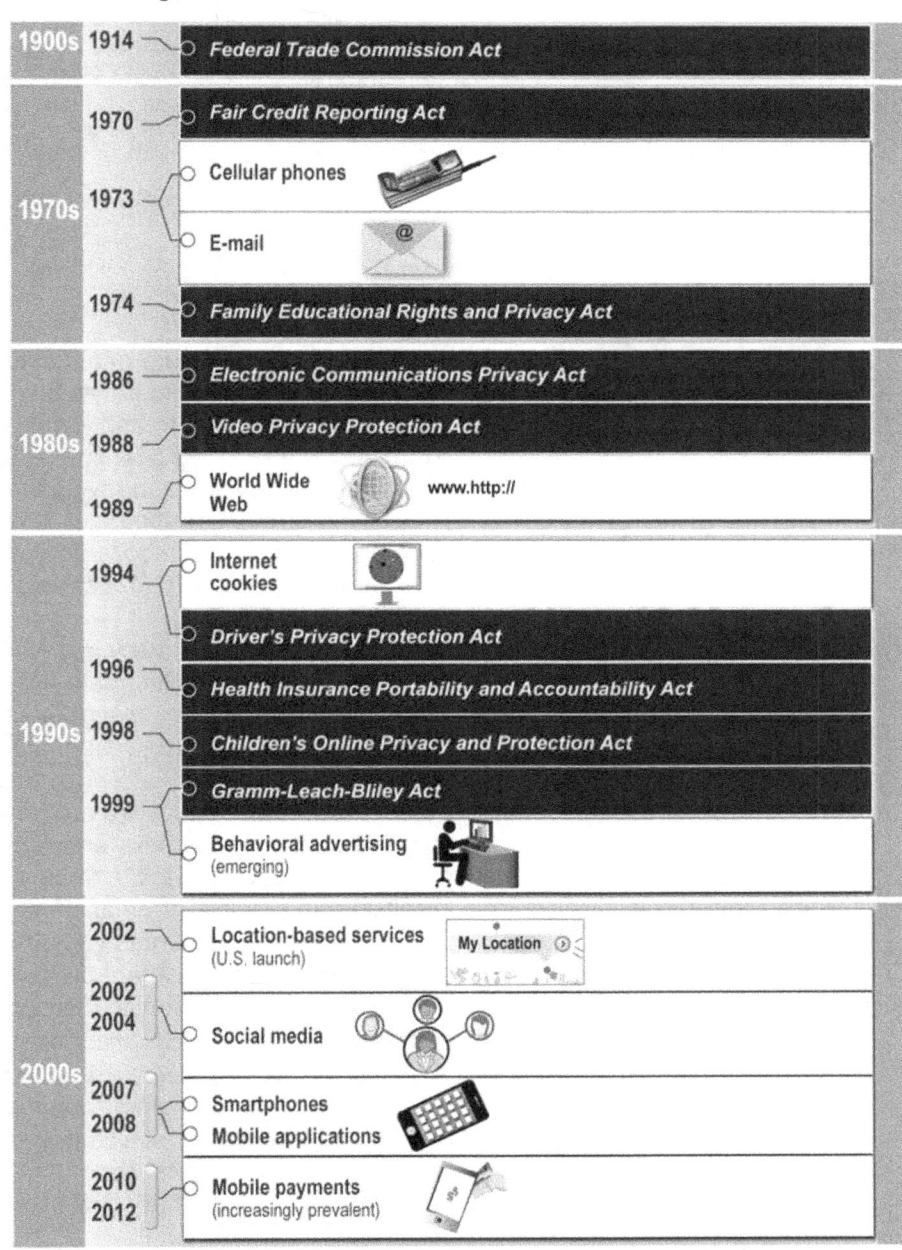

Source: GAO.

Note: The most recent amendments to the federal laws referenced in figure 2 are as follows:

- Federal Trade Commission Act of 1914: last amended on July 21, 2010 (Pub. L. 111-203).
- Fair Credit Reporting Act of 1970: last amended on Dec. 18, 2010 (Pub. L. No. 111-319).
- Family Educational Rights and Privacy Act of 1974: last amended on Jan. 14, 2013 (Pub. L. No. 112-278).
- Electronic Communications Privacy Act of 1986: last amended on Oct. 19, 2009 (Pub. L. No. 111-79).
- Video Privacy Protection Act of 1988: last amended on Jan. 10, 2013 (Pub. L. No. 112-258).
- Driver's Privacy Protection Act of 1994: last amended on Oct. 23, 2000 (Pub. L. No. 106-346).
- Health Insurance Portability and Accountability Act of 1996: last amended Mar. 23, 2010 (Pub. L. No. 111-148).
- Children's Online Privacy Protection Act of 1998: has not been amended.
- Gramm-Leach-Bliley Act of 1999: last amended on July 21, 2010 (Pub. L. No. 111-203).

Because these laws were enacted to protect the privacy of information involving specific sectors rather than address specific technologies, some have been interpreted to apply in the case of new technologies. For example, as discussed later in this report, FTC has taken enforcement activity under COPPA and revised the statute's implementing regulations to account for smartphones and mobile applications. However, online tracking practices and mobile devices remain areas in which privacy law has not fully addressed issues raised by new technologies.

Online Tracking

Currently, no federal privacy law explicitly addresses the full range of practices to track or collect data from consumers' online activity. Cookies—small text files placed on an individual computer by the website that the person visits—represent a common method of tracking online activity. The information stored in cookies allows website operators to determine whether users are repeat visitors, and allows for the recall of information users may have entered such as name and address, credit card number, site settings, and purchases in a shopping cart. Information resellers can use the information in cookies to supplement information from their databases—matching information by individuals' name and e-mail addresses—to augment profiles on individual consumers. Third parties also can synchronize their cookie files with resellers' cookie files to obtain additional information to enhance consumer profiles. Some advertisers use so-called third-party cookies—placed on a visitor's computer by a domain other than the site being visited—to track visits to the various websites on which they advertise. Although not required by law, some web browsers, such as Apple's Safari and Mozilla's Firefox, have privacy settings that allow users to block third-party cookies or turn on do-not-track features.[57] However, honoring the do-not-track setting is voluntary on the part of website operators.

Additionally, new methods of tracking consumers' online behavior seek to restrict consumers' ability to prevent such tracking. For example, according to a 2009 study, an online advertising company developed flash cookies, which combat users' ability to delete cookies.[58] Such cookies can contain up to 25 times more data than other cookies, do not expire at the end of a browsing session, and cannot be erased through web browser features such as "clear history." The study found that many popular websites, such as Google and Facebook, had been using flash cookies to recreate deleted cookies.

While current law does not explicitly address the use of web tracking, FTC has taken enforcement actions related to web tracking under its authority to enforce the prohibition of unfair or deceptive acts or practices. For example, in 2011, FTC settled charges with Google for $22.5 million after alleging that Google violated an earlier privacy settlement with FTC when it misrepresented to users of Apple's Safari web browser that it would not track and serve targeted advertisement to Safari users.[59] According to FTC, Google had placed advertising tracking cookies on individuals' computers and falsely represented that because of Safari's default settings, individuals automatically would be "opted out" of cookie tracking. Instead, Google's tracking cookies circumvented Safari's default settings, which enabled the company to use these cookies to track individuals and present them with targeted advertisements. As a result of

---

[57]For example, Safari blocks third-party cookies by default. Firefox users can approve or deny cookie storage requests and disable third-party cookies. Additionally, Safari and Firefox do-not-track features notify websites visited—and their advertisers—that web users do not want to be tracked online. Mozilla also offers a downloadable program, called Better Privacy, to combat and remove flash cookies. Finally, other companies have developed privacy and security software programs to detect and block third parties from tracking web users online.

[58]Shannon Canty, Chris Jay Hoofnagle, et al., "Flash Cookies and Privacy" (Aug. 10, 2009), available at http://papers.ssrn.com/sol3/papers.cfm?abstract_id=1446862.

[59]*United States v. Google Inc.*, No. CV 12-04177-SI, 2012 WL 5833994 (N.D. Cal. Nov. 16, 2012).

the settlement, Google agreed to disable its use of advertising tracking cookies.[60]

Federal law also does not expressly prohibit "history sniffing," which uses software code on a webpage to record the browsing history of page visitors. However, in 2012, FTC took an enforcement action against Epic Marketplace, a large online advertising network, for deceptively failing to disclose its use of history-sniffing technology.[61] The company allegedly collected data about the web sites that consumers were visiting, including sites relating to potentially sensitive topics such as impotence, menopause, disability insurance, debt relief, and personal bankruptcy. Epic Marketplace used this information to assign consumers into interest segments that were used to target advertising.

Mobile Technologies

In relation to collection and use of consumer data for marketing, no federal privacy laws that we identified specifically govern mobile applications and technologies.

Mobile applications. While various federal laws apply to activity conducted through mobile applications or mobile technologies, no federal law specifically governs mobile applications—software programs downloaded onto mobile devices for uses such as providing news and

---

[60]In December 2011, FTC finalized a settlement order with the online advertiser ScanScout, which FTC alleged deceptively had claimed that consumers could opt out of receiving targeted advertisements by changing their browser settings, whereas in fact, ScanScout used flash cookies that browser settings could not block. *In the Matter of ScanScout*, FTC File No. 102 3185, decision and order (Dec. 14, 2011). In October 2012, a web analytics company settled FTC charges that it violated the FTC Act by using web tracking software that collected personal data without disclosing the extent of information that it was collecting, *In the Matter of Compete, Inc.*, FTC File No. 102-3155, decision and order (Feb. 20, 2013).

[61]FTC alleged that Epic Marketplace's use of history-sniffing technology was deceptive because it collected data about sites outside of its network that consumers had visited, contrary to Epic's privacy policy, which represented that it would collect information only about consumers' visits to websites in its network. *In the Matter of Epic Marketplace, Inc., and Epic Media Group, LLC*, FTC File No. 112 3182, decision and order (Mar. 13, 2013).

information and online banking and shopping.[62] Application developers, operating system developers, mobile carriers, advertisers, advertising networks, and other third parties may collect an individual's information through services provided on his or her device. They may use this information to create a user profile to tailor marketing and they may sell information collected from these devices to third parties. FTC has taken enforcement action against companies for use of mobile applications that violate COPPA and FCRA.[63] The agency has taken action under the FTC Act in cases in which a mobile application developer collected or used personal information in a manner inconsistent with the application's privacy policy.[64] In addition, CFAA, which bans unauthorized access to computers, also has been found to apply to mobile phones.[65]

Location tracking. No federal privacy laws that we evaluated, with the exception of COPPA, expressly address location data, location-based technology, and consumer privacy. Smartphones and other mobile devices can provide services based on a consumer's location. We and others have reported that this capability engenders potential privacy risks, particularly if companies use or share location data without consumers'

---

[62]On July 25, 2013, the Department of Commerce released a draft of a voluntary code of conduct for mobile applications. The code sets out guidelines for short form notices that application developers and publishers can use to inform consumers about the collection and sharing of consumer information with third parties. See Department of Commerce, National Telecommunications and Information Administration, *Short Form Notice Code of Conduct To Promote Transparency In Mobile App Practices*, redline draft (July 25, 2013), available at http://www.ntia.doc.gov/files/ntia/publications/july_25_code_draft.pdf.

[63]FTC settled charges that a social networking service deceived consumers when it illegally collected information from children under 13 through its mobile application, in violation of COPPA. *See United States v. Path, Inc.*, No. C13-0448 (N.D. Cal. Jan. 31, 2013). Additionally, FTC settled charges that a company compiled and sold criminal record reports through its mobile application and operated as a consumer reporting agency, in violation of FCRA. *See In the Matter of Filiquarian Publishing, LLC*, FTC File No. 112 3195 (Apr. 30, 2013).

[64]For example, in the Path enforcement action, in addition to the alleged violation of COPPA, Path allegedly deceived users by collecting personal information from their mobile device address books without their knowledge and consent. *See United States v. Path, Inc.*, No. C13-0448 (N.D. Cal. Jan. 31, 2013).

[65]In 2011, the U.S. Court of Appeals for the Eighth Circuit held that a basic cellular telephone—used only to place calls and send text messages—was a computer for the purposes of CFAA. The judicial decision did not address more advanced devices, such as smartphones, in the CFAA context. *See U.S. v. Kramer*, 631 F.3d 900 (8th Cir. 2011).

knowledge.[66] In 2010, Commerce recommended that the Administration review ECPA to address privacy protection of location-based services.[67] As noted previously, ECPA generally prohibits the interception and disclosure of individuals' electronic communications, but this may not apply if location data were not deemed content. ECPA also would not govern the interception or access of information transmitted and stored by entities not covered by ECPA, which typically would include developers of location-based applications. However, COPPA regulations govern the collection of geolocation data sufficient to identify street name and the name of a city or town from children under 13, and FTC could pursue enforcement action if a location-based provider's collection or use of geolocation information violated COPPA.

Mobile payments. No federal privacy laws that we evaluated expressly address mobile payments. Such services, which allow individuals to transfer money or pay for goods and services using their mobile devices, have become increasingly prevalent. According to a survey conducted by the Board of Governors of the Federal Reserve System, 6 percent of smartphone users used their telephones at cash registers to pay for purchases in 2012.[68] A 2013 report by FTC noted that although mobile payment can be an easy and convenient way for individuals to pay for goods and services, privacy concerns have arisen because of the number of companies involved in the mobile payment marketplace and the large

---

[66]In 2012, we reported that the risks of mobile technologies included disclosure to third parties for unspecified uses, the tracking of consumer behavior (location tracking can be combined with tracking of online activity), and identity theft. For example, criminals can use disclosed location and other sensitive information to steal identities. See GAO, *Mobile Device Location ID: Additional Federal Actions Could Help Protect Consumer Privacy*, GAO-12-903 (Washington, D.C.: Sept. 11, 2012). A Federal Communications Commission report also noted privacy risks, particularly because numerous third parties can access consumers' personal information through location-based applications. See Federal Communications Commission, *Location-Based Services: An Overview of Opportunities and Other Considerations* (Washington, D.C.: May 2012).

[67]See Department of Commerce, Internet Policy Task Force, *Commercial Data Privacy and Innovation in the Internet Economy: A Dynamic Policy Framework* (Washington, D.C.: December 2010).

[68]Board of Governors of the Federal Reserve System, *Consumers and Mobile Financial Services 2013* (Washington, D.C.: March 2013).

amount of detailed personal and purchase information collected and consolidated in the process.[69]

Views Differ on Whether Existing Legal Framework Has Gaps and If Legislation Is Needed to Improve Privacy Protections

Stakeholder views have diverged on whether significant gaps in the current legal framework for privacy exist, whether more legislation is needed, or whether self-regulation can suffice.

Extent of Gaps in Existing Privacy Framework

The marketing and information reseller industries generally have argued that the current framework of sector-specific laws and regulations has not left significant gaps in consumer privacy protections, citing several reasons. First, they have stated that the list of federal and state laws regulating uses of personal information is extensive. Second, some industry representatives have stated that the existing legislative and regulatory framework generally provides adequate privacy protections— or the flexibility to address such protections—in relation to new technologies.[70] For example, they have noted that the FTC Act grants FTC broad authority that can apply to a range of circumstances and technologies—as with the enforcement actions discussed earlier to address alleged misrepresentations of a company's privacy policy involving web tracking and history sniffing. Third, a representative of one reseller said that any gaps that might exist in consumer privacy protection were a result of gaps in enforcement of existing law rather than in the legal framework itself. Finally, some have asserted that consumers' expectations and notion of privacy have changed in the technological age—for example, many consumers voluntarily share private information in public online settings—which may mitigate the need for strict privacy controls mandated by law that would apply to all consumers.

[69]Federal Trade Commission, *Paper, Plastic or Mobile? An FTC Workshop on Mobile Payments* (Washington, D.C.: March 2013).

[70]For example, Senate Committee on Commerce, Science, and Transportation, *Privacy and Data Security: Protecting Consumers in a Modern World*, 112th Cong., 1st sess., June 29, 2011; see testimony of Stuart Pratt, Consumer Data Industry Association.

In contrast, privacy advocates and others have stated that the current privacy scheme left significant gaps. In July 2010 testimony, one privacy advocate said that the current legal framework for privacy consisted of "a confusing patchwork of distinct standards" that resulted in gaps in privacy protection.[71] In a July 2011 letter to members of Congress, privacy advocates and consumer organizations stated that the current legal framework for privacy was inadequate, largely because laws had not been updated to address privacy challenges arising from technological developments.[72] Similarly, in public comments received by Commerce in 2010, some who commented suggested that changes in technology and business models rendered parts of the U.S. privacy policy framework out of date. Commerce noted in its privacy report that many of the key actors in the Internet age—including online advertisers and their data sources, cloud computing and location-based services, and social networks— operated without specific statutory obligations to protect personal data.[73] Additionally, we have raised concerns about the relevance of the current privacy framework in relation to the vast increases in the volume of personal information collected and shared.[74]

Legislation versus Self-Regulation

Industry and privacy advocates also have disagreed on the need for more legislation or regulation and the efficacy of self-regulatory approaches to protect privacy. Industry representatives have acknowledged the importance of consumer privacy protections, but generally argued that voluntary industry measures and self-regulation have mitigated the need for additional privacy legislation. The Direct Marketing Association issued Guidelines for Ethical Business Practice that include principles of conduct

[71]House Committee on Energy and Commerce, Subcommittee on Commerce, Trade, and Consumer Protection, *The Best Practices Act of 2010 and Other Federal Privacy Legislation,* 111th Cong., 2nd sess., July 22, 2010; see testimony of Leslie Harris, President and Chief Executive Officer, Center for Democracy and Technology.

[72]Letter of consumer and privacy organizations to Senate Committee on Commerce, Science, and Transportation (July 1, 2011).

[73]Commerce, *Commercial Data Privacy and Innovation in the Internet Economy* (2010).

[74]GAO-06-674.

for its members.[75] And, as discussed earlier in this report, the Digital Advertising Alliance has implemented a program related to online behavioral advertising that provides consumers some control over their information online.[76] At a recent Senate hearing, a representative of the alliance stated that industry self-regulation was flexible and could adapt to rapid changes in technology and consumer expectations, whereas legislation and government regulation could be inflexible and quickly become outdated in an era of rapidly evolving technologies.[77] Moreover, the representative said that the self-regulatory program was backed by robust industry enforcement mechanisms. Similarly, in June 2011, a number of trade associations and business groups sent a letter to Congress urging caution as Congress examined whether changes were necessary to existing privacy laws.[78] The letter argued that absent any identifiable harm in the marketplace, privacy issues were best addressed through industry self-regulatory programs and best practices. Specifically, the letter noted that self-regulation and best business practices that were technology-neutral serve as the preferred framework for enhancing investment and competition while—at the same time—protecting consumers' privacy. Other stakeholders have testified that imposing privacy protections by law or regulation—rather than through self-regulatory means—would raise compliance costs for businesses, with these increased costs falling hardest on small operators and start-up

---

[75]Direct Marketing Association, *Guidelines for Ethical Business Practice*, available at http://dmaresponsibility.org. The principles require that association members (1) maintain appropriate security policies and practices to safeguard information, (2) provide information on association policies about the transfer of personally identifiable information for marketing purposes, and (3) honor requests not to have personally identifiable information transferred for marketing purposes.

[76]In July 2013, the Digital Advertising Alliance issued guidance as to how its principles apply in mobile environments, including mobile websites and applications.

[77]Senate Committee on Commerce, Science, and Transportation, *The Need for Privacy Protections: Is Industry Self-Regulation Adequate?*, 112th Cong., 2nd sess., June 28, 2012; see testimony of Robert Liodice, President and Chief Executive Officer, Association of National Advertisers, Inc. on behalf of the Digital Advertising Alliance.

[78]U.S. Chamber of Commerce, letter on changes to privacy law, available at http://uschamber.com/issues/letters/2011/multiindustry-letter-changes-privacy-law.

companies.[79] (We discuss views about the economic effects of enhanced regulatory protections in more detail later in this report.)

In contrast, some privacy advocates and others have argued that voluntary compliance or self-regulation is not sufficient to uniformly protect consumer privacy rights. The World Privacy Forum issued a report in 2011 stating that a majority of industry self-regulatory programs were inadequate in protecting consumer privacy and failed in one or more substantive ways.[80] For example, the report asserted that self-regulatory organizations formed their programs in secret, that the programs covered only a fraction of an industry or an industry subgroup, and that self-regulatory organizations lacked the ability to enforce the guidelines or practices among members. The Privacy Forum report cited examples of self-regulatory efforts that were no longer in existence, such as the Individual Reference Services Group.[81] One academic privacy scholar has argued that self-regulation largely affirms industry's current and prospective business practices, creates only narrow rights for consumers, and does not cover new actors that may fall outside of the industry's self-regulatory regime.[82] The Privacy Rights Clearinghouse has argued that self-regulation is ineffective because some companies use the "notice-and-choice model." That is, they provide consumers with privacy policies describing their data collection and use practices, but these policies are often lengthy and dense, and consumers typically do not read or use them to make informed choices. The organization has said that many information resellers and other companies do little to inform consumers or provide them with choices on the collection, handling, or disposition of their data.

---

[79]Senate Committee, *A Status Update on the Development of Voluntary Do-Not-Track Standards,* April 24, 2013; see testimony of Adam Thierer, Senior Research Fellow, Mercatus Center, George Mason University. House Subcommittee, *HR 5777, the Best Practices Act,* July 22, 2010; see testimony of Jason Goldman, Counsel, U.S. Chamber of Commerce.

[80]Robert Gellman and Pam Dixon, "Many Failures: A Brief History of Privacy Self-Regulation in the United States" (World Privacy Forum: Oct. 14, 2011).

[81]According to the report, the Individual Reference Services Group (a self-regulatory organization formed in 1997 for companies providing information that identifies or locates individuals) ceased functioning in 2001 because it said self-regulation was no longer necessary due to the enactment of the Gramm-Leach-Bliley Act.

[82]Chris Hoofnagle, "Can Privacy Self-Regulation Work for Consumers?" available at http://techpolicy.com/CanPrivacySelf-RegulationWork-Hoofnagle.aspx.

In its March 2012 report on consumer privacy, FTC said that self-regulation could play an important role in consumer privacy but said that there had been little self-regulation to date and it had not gone far enough. In particular, FTC said that efforts by the information reseller industry to establish self-regulatory rules on consumer privacy had fallen short, noting that basic privacy concepts like transparency about the nature of companies' data practices and meaningful consumer control were absent. The report acknowledged that imposing new privacy protections would result in costs for industry, but said that additional protections also would build consumer trust in the marketplace, which in turn would benefit businesses. FTC's report urged industry to accelerate the pace of self-regulation and made several recommendations for businesses aimed at increasing consumer choice and control and helping to promote privacy protection.

Views Differ on Specific versus Comprehensive Approaches to Privacy Law and on Consumer Interests

In addition to the differing views on whether to impose additional legislative or regulatory privacy protections, debate has focused on the appropriate approach for any such legislation or regulation. In general, this debate can be framed around three sets of issues, addressed below: (1) a comprehensive versus sector-specific approach to privacy legislation; (2) how to address consumers' interests in accessing, controlling, and correcting their data; and (3) the potential impact of new regulation on consumers and commerce.

Views on a Comprehensive versus Sector-Specific Approach to Privacy Legislation

Debate has been ongoing about what kind of legislative approach—sectoral or comprehensive—would best effect enhanced consumer privacy protections. As discussed previously, instead of being governed by a comprehensive law that sets a baseline for privacy protections, privacy in the United States is governed through a framework of subject-specific laws that apply to discreet economic sectors and protect selected types and uses of consumers' personal data. Such a framework is relatively rare among nations; according to Commerce, many countries have comprehensive privacy models under a single legal framework.

While not recommending a comprehensive federal privacy statute per se, in 2010 Commerce's Internet Policy Task Force recommended the adoption of a baseline commercial data privacy framework built on an expanded set of the FIPPs. The task force's report solicited public comment on whether these baseline privacy principles should be enacted by statute or through other means.[83] The report noted that adopting baseline FIPPs would help fill gaps in current data privacy protections that resulted from the current sectoral approach. Moreover, it noted that a FIPPs-based framework might be more suitable for applying privacy principles that could adapt to future changes in technology and other conditions.

The 2012 White House privacy framework called on Congress to enact baseline privacy legislation while also preserving existing sector-specific laws. The Administration noted that the existing framework for consumer data privacy in the United States was flexible and effectively addressed some consumer data privacy challenges in the digital age. At the same time, it noted that much of the personal data used on the Internet was not subject to comprehensive federal statutory protection and that there was a need to fill gaps across the range of environments in which individuals have access to networked technologies. It said that baseline consumer data privacy legislation that implemented the framework's Consumer Bill of Rights would provide a level playing field for companies, a consistent set of expectations for consumers, and greater clarity and transparency about the basis for FTC enforcement actions. At the same time, the Administration argued that existing federal data privacy laws, such as HIPAA and FCRA, provide effective and well-tailored privacy protections. To avoid creating duplicative regulatory burdens, the Administration supported exempting companies from consumer data privacy legislation to the extent that their activities were subject to existing federal data privacy laws. Thus, it said that baseline legislation would preserve existing sector-specific federal laws that effectively protect personal data, minimize the duplication of legal requirements, and provide consumers with a clear sense of what protections they have and who enforces them. FTC's March 2012 privacy report also expressly called on Congress to consider enacting baseline privacy legislation, while also urging industry to accelerate self-regulation.

---

[83]Department of Commerce, *Notice of Inquiry: Information Privacy and Innovation in the Internet Economy.*

Potential Advantages of Comprehensive Privacy Legislation

Some consumer and privacy groups and academic experts have cited what they believe are several advantages to comprehensive privacy legislation. First, they have said that only baseline legislation would fill gaps in existing privacy protections and provide comprehensive consumer privacy protections. Some consumer and privacy advocates argued that the current sectoral privacy framework has produced highly uneven results and many gaps in coverage. For example, the Center for Democracy and Technology has noted that while strong privacy laws for cable viewing and video records exist, the collection and use of much of the data held by smartphone applications is subject only to Section 5 of the FTC Act, which prohibits unfair or deceptive acts or practices in or affecting commerce.[84] Second, some advocates say that a comprehensive law would offer uniformity—providing privacy protections to consumers on a more reliable and consistent basis in a variety of contexts. Comprehensive legislation also could create more uniformity to the extent that it preempted state laws that were inconsistent with federal policy.

Privacy advocates and some business representatives also have argued that comprehensive privacy legislation would be beneficial for businesses. In congressional testimony in 2010, one consumer advocate said that the lack of comprehensive privacy protections put U.S. companies at a disadvantage overseas because many foreign companies and governments were uncomfortable with, or in some cases legally restricted from, engaging in business with them.[85] One industry representative also has suggested that comprehensive privacy legislation could help reduce compliance costs because the current sectoral approach, with multiple laws, makes compliance a complex and costly task for many organizations. FTC noted in its 2012 privacy report that some business representatives noted in public comments that baseline privacy legislation would help provide legal certainty and serve as a key mechanism for building trust among customers.[86]

---

[84]House Subcommittee, *HR 5777, the Best Practices Act*, July 22, 2010; see testimony of Leslie Harris, President and Chief Executive Officer, Center for Democracy and Technology.

[85]Testimony of Leslie Harris, July 22, 2010.

[86]Federal Trade Commission, *Protecting Consumer Privacy in an Era of Rapid Change: A Proposed Framework for Businesses and Policymakers* (March 2012), p. 11. Available at http://ftc.gov/os/2012/03/120326privacyreport.pdf.

GAO-13-663 Information Resellers

Potential Disadvantages of Comprehensive Privacy Legislation

Industry stakeholders have argued a comprehensive privacy law would amount to a one-size-fits-all approach to regulation, which could be overly burdensome because no single law can be tailored to fit the practices of each individual company and industry. For example, one information reseller told us comprehensive baseline privacy legislation might not make distinctions between types of and uses for personal data and said that data used for marketing purposes generally were more benign and thus the threshold for privacy protections should be lower for these purposes.

Stakeholders also said that the current sector-specific system was well-suited to addressing those gaps—for example through targeted rulemaking or legislation that sought to address a specific new technology or sector not adequately covered under current law. Moreover, they said that a sector-specific approach provided greater flexibility to tailor appropriate restrictions based on the types and uses of data. Some industry representatives note that FCRA has been successful in providing appropriate privacy protections tailored to specific types of data (those used for certain eligibility determinations) that can be particularly sensitive because they can affect a consumer's ability to get credit, insurance, or employment.

Other stakeholders also suggested refinements to existing sector-specific laws. An information reseller with whom we spoke suggested that a preferred alternative to implementing a comprehensive or baseline federal privacy law would be to create more consistency in definitions and approaches among the current sector-specific privacy laws. One privacy advocate with whom we spoke said that because comprehensive privacy legislation may be politically unfeasible, it may be beneficial instead to focus on strengthening, extending, and updating existing sector-specific legislation such as FCRA and HIPAA.

Views on How to Address Consumers' Interests in the Use of and Control of Their Data

Other debate on privacy protections has focused on the third-party market for and usage of consumer data, whether or how consumers can access and control such usage or correct the data, and how or if limits should apply to web tracking.

Use of Consumer Data

Changes in the marketplace for consumer data include a vast increase in recent years in the number and types of companies that collect and share such data with third parties. FTC has noted a distinction between first-party data—data held by the party that originally requested or collected it—and third-party data—data purchased or otherwise obtained by a third party, often to be used for a purpose different than originally intended.[87] For example, as noted earlier, information from a retail store purchase or a warranty registration card can be sold to a third party to be used for marketing purposes. In the online environment, consumers who provide their e-mail addresses and other personal information for a nonmarketing purpose to a website may find that information sold to an advertising network or data aggregator for purposes unrelated to that website. Some information resellers may use the information that was provided to determine the consumer's identity and associated demographic information, which can be used to customize future advertising, all without the consumer's awareness. In some cases, the information could be sensitive—for example, activity on a health-related website that results in the collection and use of information about a consumer's interest in a particular medical topic.

In a July 2010 testimony, a representative of one consumer advocacy organization proposed certain limitations on the use of personal data for purposes beyond which the data were provided. He noted that consumers face obstacles in understanding how and why their information is being collected, analyzed, and used, and that they cannot rely on privacy policies and disclosures to provide clear disclosure or consent to repurposing of a consumer's information.[88] Representatives of two privacy advocacy organizations with whom we spoke similarly noted that consumers often were not aware of, and had not always consented to, personal information being repurposed for marketing and other uses.

In its 2012 privacy framework, the Administration noted that consumers have a right to expect that companies will collect, use, and disclose their information in ways that are consistent with the context in which the information was provided.[89] That is, companies should limit their use and disclosure to those purposes consistent with the relationship that they have with consumers and the context in which consumers originally disclosed the information. In addition, it noted that if companies used or

---

[87]Federal Trade Commission, *Protecting Consumer Privacy in an Era of Rapid Change,* pp. 42-44.

[88]House Subcommittee on Commerce, Trade, and Consumer Protection, *HR 5777, The Best Practices Act,* 111th Cong., 2nd sess., July 22, 2010; see testimony of Edmund Mierzwinski, U.S. PIRG Consumer Program Director.

[89]The White House, *A Framework for Protecting Privacy* (2012).

disclosed the information for other purposes, they should provide transparency and choice by disclosing those other purposes in a manner that is prominent and easily understandable to consumers. In its 2012 privacy report, FTC articulated a "context of the interaction" standard for determining when a practice required consumer choice. Under this standard, a requirement for consumer choice would depend on the extent to which the practice was consistent with the context of the transaction or the consumer's existing relationship with the business, or was required or specifically authorized by law.[90]

Representatives of information resellers, marketers, and other industries that use consumer data have argued that repurposing of consumer information generally is not inappropriate or harmful. According to one reseller with whom we spoke, personal information that consumers provide to unrestricted websites—such as certain social media sites, blogs, or discussion boards—becomes publicly available information, and therefore can be used by a third party for various purposes, without any legal or ethical limitations on its use. Other industry representatives have noted that companies often clearly disclose to consumers that information consumers provide may be used for marketing purposes. For example, some resellers with whom we spoke said that disclosure on how personal information may be used generally was given when consumers provided personal information through such venues as loyalty card programs, contests and surveys, and website and warranty registrations. However, they acknowledged that some consumers might not read these disclosures. In addition, some industry representatives have noted that information resellers avoid web extraction in most cases and that some forms of web scraping violate the Direct Marketing Association's mandatory ethical standards, which prohibit a company from selling or sharing personally identifiable information obtained from social media channels or online referral marketing without prior permission from the referred individuals.

Access and Correction

Stakeholders' views have differed on the extent to which consumers should be able to access data held about them. In its 2012 report, FTC said that companies should provide reasonable access to the consumer data they maintain, a position that many privacy groups have echoed.

---

[90]Federal Trade Commission, *Protecting Consumer Privacy in an Era of Rapid Change,* pp. 38-39.

The agency noted that consumer access rights should be proportional to the sensitivity and the intended use of the data at issue—for example, consumers typically would have less access to data held about them for marketing purposes than they would for data covered under FCRA and used for eligibility determinations. FTC called on information resellers that compile data for marketing purposes to explore creating a centralized website where resellers would identify themselves and describe how they collect and use consumer data, and the access rights and other choices that consumers have. Some industry representatives with whom we spoke said that such a centralized website would serve to confuse most consumers and be costly to businesses. Representatives of two privacy advocacy groups noted that while a centralized website would encourage transparency, it likely would not provide consumers with comprehensive or meaningful information. FTC staff told us that the agency has been discussing the feasibility of such a centralized website with stakeholders.

Debate also has developed on consumers' right to correct information held about them for marketing purposes. As noted earlier, no federal law that we examined gives consumers the right to correct or delete inaccurate, incomplete, or unverifiable information used for marketing or look-up purposes not covered by FCRA. Some privacy advocates and members of Congress have argued that consumers should have the inherent right to correct inaccurate information about them that is being held and sold. In addition, one privacy advocate noted that uses of data not covered by FCRA can include fraud prevention and identity verification, and that inaccuracies in these databases can cause inconvenience or harm to a consumer. For data used for marketing, another privacy advocate has noted that companies may base some individual product pricing on a consumer's profile, so inaccurate data could affect the price offered. However, both FTC and the Direct Marketing Association have expressed the belief that special measures are not needed to ensure the accuracy of data maintained and used for marketing purposes because the only resulting harm to consumers might be to receive irrelevant advertising.[91] The Administration expressed a similar view in its 2012 privacy framework, which noted that in providing consumers the opportunity to correct inaccurate data, companies may consider the scale, scope, and sensitivity of the data and whether

---

[91]Federal Trade Commission, *Protecting Consumer Privacy in an Era of Rapid Change*, pp. 38-39; and letter from Direct Marketing Association to members of Congress on August 13, 2012, available at http://the-dma.org/news/August-13-2012-DMALetter.pdf.

consumers would be exposed to any financial, physical, or other material harm if the data were inaccurate. In addition, some resellers have stated that because they acquire information continuously from a variety of sources, providing consumers with an opportunity to correct erroneous information would not be effective unless consumers also corrected the information at the sources from which it had been drawn.

Web Tracking

Some of the most publicized debate related to privacy and new technologies has been on the issue of consumers' ability to control the tracking of their web activity. Areas of disagreement include the effectiveness of voluntary initiatives that currently allow consumers to exert some control over web tracking and the use of information collected during such tracking. The Digital Advertising Alliance maintains a website (http://aboutads.info/choices) that allows consumers to opt out of behavioral advertising by its participating companies. The alliance also developed an icon to let web page users know that their visit to that page was being tracked and their actions used to infer their interests and target future advertising. Users can click the icon to learn more about behavioral advertising and control whether they receive such advertising and from which companies.[92] The Digital Advertising Alliance said it believes that these initiatives provide consumers with meaningful and effective choice tools. However, some privacy advocates have pointed to limitations to this mechanism, noting that the opt-out option focuses on what behavioral advertising consumers see rather than the extent to which their web habits are tracked. In addition, the option applies only to companies that are participants of the Digital Advertising Alliance, although the alliance notes that this includes most online advertising networks.

Debate also has developed in recent years about the implementation of "do not track," another method for facilitating consumer choice. Under this approach, consumers would be able to choose whether to allow the collection and use of data about their online searching and browsing activities (through cookies or other mechanisms). Typically, this would involve the placement of a "flag" on the consumer's browser signaling the consumer's choices for tracking and receiving targeted advertisements. FTC supported the concept of a universal "do not track" mechanism in its 2010 and 2012 privacy reports, noting that it could be accomplished

---

[92]According to the Digital Advertising Alliance, in 2012 more than 5.2 million unique users accessed the resources at www.aboutads.info, and nearly 1 million exercised a choice using the site's opt-out mechanism.

either through legislation or through robust, enforceable self-regulation.[93] On the self-regulatory side, some Internet browsers, including Mozilla Firefox, have introduced do-not-track features. The World Wide Web Consortium has been developing a universal web protocol for "do not track."[94] Disagreements among stakeholders on a number of different issues (such as scope, technological specifications, and which parties should respond to a request) have delayed widespread adoption or standardization of "do not track."[95]

Additionally, various proposals have been made in Congress and elsewhere that would require FTC to promulgate regulations to implement a "do not track" mechanism.[96] Although the specific methods and parameters of the proposals vary widely, proponents have made several general assertions in their favor. They note that the use of third-party cookies and behavioral advertising greatly increased in recent years—for example, the Wall Street Journal identified more than 3,000 tracking files placed on a test computer by the top 50 websites.[97] Advocacy organizations such as the Center for Democracy and Technology have argued that Internet users may not be fully aware of the extent of such tracking by third parties and that users should have to affirmatively consent to the tracking of their online behavior. Some members of

---

[93]Federal Trade Commission, *Protecting Consumer Privacy in an Era of Rapid Change (2012)* and *Protecting Consumer Privacy in an Era of Rapid Change: A Proposed Framework for Businesses and Policymakers;* preliminary staff report (Washington, D.C.: December 2010).

[94]In the World Wide Web Consortium, member organizations and the public work together to develop web protocols and standards. The consortium's Tracking Protection Working Group is responsible for proposing recommendations and technologies to improve user privacy and control by expressing preferences for blocking or allowing web tracking. See http://w3.org/2011/tracking-protection/.

[95]Senate Committee on Commerce, Science, and Transportation, *A Status Update on the Development of Voluntary Do-Not-Track Standards*, 113th Cong., 1st sess., April 24, 2013; see testimony of Justin Brookman, Director, Consumer Privacy, Center for Democracy and Technology.

[96]For example, see the *Do Not Track Me Online Act*, H.R. 654, 112th Cong., 1st session. The bill was referred to committee on February 11, 2011, where it died. See the *Do-Not-Track Online Act of 2011*, S. 913, 112th Cong., 1st session. The bill was referred to committee on May 9, 2011, where it died. See *also*, *Do-Not-Track Online Act of 2013*, S. 418, 113th Cong., 1st session. The bill was referred to committee on February 28, 2013.

[97]Julia Angwin, "The Web's New Gold Mine: Your Secrets," *Wall Street Journal*, July 30, 2010.

Congress also have raised concerns about supercookies (that is, flash cookies) and whether these would be covered by the prohibition of unfair or deceptive acts or practices in Section 5 of the FTC Act.

Representatives of the advertising and some other industries have cautioned against many of the proposals for a do-not-track mandate. The Digital Advertising Alliance has argued that the current opt-out mechanism it provides is an effective means for consumers to control the collection and use of their web viewing data, and that such self-regulation is a more flexible and efficient approach than legislative mandate.[98] Industry representatives also have asserted that limiting consumer web tracking could adversely affect consumers' online experiences—for example, by not facilitating advertising relevant to their interests or reducing advertising revenues used to provide free content.

Views on the Potential Impact of New Regulation on Consumers and Commerce

Benefits of Information Sharing for Consumers

Representatives of the marketing and reseller industries have argued that regulatory restrictions on the use of consumer data unintentionally could reduce the benefits consumers reap from the use and sharing of personal information. First, advertising representatives have noted that marketing and advertising that can be targeted to individual consumers helps underwrite the cost of web applications and online services that are available free to consumers.[99] Second, the ability to collect and share personal information has resulted in many products and services that are useful or enjoyable to consumers. For example, representatives of individual reference (look-up) sites have noted that their products allow users to reconnect with friends and family members or learn more about prospective romantic partners. Similarly, representatives of leading Internet service providers have noted that location-based services such

---

[98]Senate Committee, *A Status Update on the Development of Voluntary Do-Not-Track Standards*, April 24, 2013; see testimony of Luigi Mastria, Managing Director, Digital Advertising Alliance.

[99]House Subcommittee, *H.R. 5777, The Best Practices Act,* July 22, 2010; see testimony of Michael Zaneis, Vice President of Public Policy, Interactive Advertising Bureau.

as those available on mobile devices can offer a vastly improved user experience when the user reveals his or her current position. Third, some resellers have said that consumers benefit from targeted behavioral advertising because it provides them with information about products and services relevant to their specific interests, needs, or preferences—all at a time when the consumer is likely interested in such products or services. A 2013 poll commissioned by the Digital Advertising Alliance found that about 68 percent of respondents indicated they would prefer that at least some of the Internet advertisements they saw were directed toward their interests, compared with about 16 percent who preferred to see random advertisements.[100] The U.S. Chamber of Commerce has noted that public policymakers must consider benefits to consumers in weighing the trade-offs between protection of privacy rights and other factors.[101]

However, some privacy advocates expressed the belief that the benefits to consumers have been overstated and were skeptical that most consumers highly desired targeted advertising. Some advocates also raised concerns that the profiling and scoring techniques used to deliver specific advertisements to specific consumers might have discriminatory effects because they presented information, sales, or opportunities only to consumers with certain characteristics.

Innovation and Economic Benefits

Stakeholder views again diverged in relation to the potential economic effects of strengthened privacy regulations. The Direct Marketing Association and other industry representatives have said that companies' ability to readily collect, use, and share consumer information has had economic benefits and fostered innovation that could be inhibited by legislative proposals or regulation that restricted the collection and use of this information. In 2010, commercial and nonprofit marketers spent about $154 billion on direct marketing advertising expenditures, according to the

---

[100]In addition, approximately 16 percent said they were not sure. The poll surveyed 1,000 likely voters nationwide on April 2-3, 2013. Slight weights were added to age, race, gender, region, party, education, and religion to more accurately reflect the population. Zogby Analytics, *Interactive Survey of U.S. Adults,* commissioned by the Digital Advertising Alliance (2013), available at http://www.aboutads.info/resource/image/Poll/Zogby_DAA_Poll.pdf.

[101]House Subcommittee, *HR 5777, the Best Practices Act,* July 22, 2010; see testimony of Jason Goldman, Counsel for Telecommunications and E-Commerce, U.S. Chamber of Commerce.

Direct Marketing Association, accounting for about 51 percent of all advertising expenditures in the United States.[102] Additionally, industry representatives have noted that the Internet has become an increasingly important part of the U.S. economy—for example, retail e-commerce sales totaled about $225 billion in 2012, according to Commerce—and data-driven marketing helped facilitate this activity. According to a study by the Network Advertising Initiative, behaviorally targeted advertising generated almost three times more revenue and was twice as effective at converting browsers into buyers than nontargeted online advertising.[103] According to a study commissioned by the Interactive Advertising Bureau—an organization of media and technology companies engaging in online advertising—advertising-supported Internet activity that uses consumer data has significant economic benefits, including job creation.[104]

In addition, representatives of the information reseller industry have said that the use of consumer information for data-driven marketing helps to foster competition online and ensures that large and small businesses can reach consumers across the Internet. According to a 2011 study by a global consulting firm, the availability of consumer data has enabled much of recent economic innovation and growth.[105] For example, the study cited the emergence of real-time location data as creating an entirely new set of location-based services, from navigation applications to people tracking. In a 2013 congressional hearing, representatives of two industry

---

[102]Direct Marketing Association, *The Power of Direct Marketing: ROI, Sales, Expenditures, and Employment in the U.S.*, 2011-2012 edition (New York, N.Y., October 2011), pp. 31 and 239.

[103]Howard Beales, "The Value of Behavioral Targeting," March 24, 2010, available at http://www.networkadvertising.org/pdfs/Beales_NAI_Study.pdf.

[104]Hamilton Consultants, Inc., John Deighton, and John Quelch, "Economic Value of the Advertising-Supported Internet Ecosystem" (Cambridge, Mass.: June 10, 2009), available at http://iab.net/media/file/Economic-Value-Report.pdf. The study estimated that the Internet created more than 1.2 million new jobs—including jobs that conduct advertising and commerce on the Internet—in the United States over the last 10-15 years.

[105]James Manyika, Michael Chui, et al., *Big Data—The Next Frontier for Innovation, Competition, and Productivity*, May 2011, available at http://mckinsey.com/insights/business_technology/big_data_the_next_frontier_for_innovation.

associations stated that stricter privacy controls would increase compliance costs for businesses, particularly smaller businesses.[106]

However, privacy and consumer groups generally have argued that even with restrictions on the use of consumer data, industries that use such data would find a way to expand their businesses and remain profitable. They noted that the industry's claims that increased privacy protections would be too burdensome and stifle innovation have not been accompanied by convincing evidence. Moreover, some privacy and consumer groups have stated that effective privacy regulations actually can have positive effects on the economy and innovation. They noted that privacy-enhancing technology, such as data encryption, that safeguards personal information online has led to greater consumer participation online, including more e-commerce.[107] They also argued that enhanced privacy protections may encourage companies to develop innovative services that rely less on personal information. The White House privacy framework noted that consumers who feel protected from misuse of their personal information likely would be more open to engaging in commerce and various online technologies. Privacy advocates have cited the example of encryption technology to enable secure online payments as increasing consumers' willingness to engage in online financial transactions.[108] In addition, one privacy organization noted that competition among companies to address consumers' privacy concerns could encourage innovations.[109]

---

[106]Senate Committee, *A Status Update on the Development of Voluntary Do-Not-Track Standards,* April 24, 2013; see testimony of Luigi Mastria, Managing Director, Digital Advertising Alliance, and testimony of Adam Thierer, Senior Research Fellow, Mercatus Center, George Mason University.

[107]See letter of consumer and privacy organizations. Industry representatives also have ta ked about the importance of consumer trust. For example, in *A Status Update on the Development of Voluntary Do-Not-Track Standards,* April 24, 2013; see testimony of Harvey Anderson, Senior Vice President Business and Legal Affairs, Mozilla.

[108]Department of Commerce, *Notice of Inquiry: Information Privacy and Innovation in the Internet Economy,* 75 Fed. Reg. 80042, Dec. 21, 2010. Notice and all comments are available at http://ntia.doc.gov/federal-register-notices/2010/information-privacy-and-innovation-internet-economy-notice. See comments of the Electronic Privacy Information Center at pp. 13-14; and comments of Consumer Watchdog at p. 3.

[109]See http://ntia.doc.gov/federal-register-notices/2010/information-privacy-and-innovation-internet-economy-notice comments of the Electronic Privacy Information Center at pp. 13-14.

Similarly, the Federal Communications Commission stated in a 2012 report that companies that could demonstrate clear and consistent transparency in collection and use of personal information could be competitive and more attractive to consumers.[110] In public comments solicited by Commerce in 2010 on information privacy and innovation in the Internet economy, online businesses and advertisers noted the importance of respecting customers' privacy if they wanted to retain their business, and information and communications technology companies stated that privacy protections were necessary to encourage individuals to adopt new devices and services.[111] According to a representative of one privacy organization, even in those cases in which privacy regulations served to inhibit one line of marketing—as with the effect on telemarketers of regulation creating the National Do Not Call Registry—advertisers and marketers have been able to rapidly shift to other profitable marketing avenues.[112]

International Harmonization

Views vary on the economic effects of greater harmonization of U.S. privacy rules with those of our trading partners. One of the recommendations of Commerce's Internet Policy Task Force in 2010 was that the U.S. government should increase cooperation with other countries' privacy enforcement authorities and work toward mutual recognition of other commercial data privacy frameworks.[113] The task force noted that a significant number of stakeholders from whom they solicited comments noted difficulties in complying with multiple foreign data protection rules and regulations. These difficulties included restrictions on transferring data between jurisdictions and significant costs

---

[110]See Federal Communications Commission, Wireless Telecommunications Bureau, *Location-Based Services: An Overview of Opportunities and Other Considerations* (Washington, D.C.: May 2012).

[111]Department of Commerce, Notice of Inquiry, Information Privacy and Innovation in the Internet Economy (Privacy and Innovation NOI), 75 Fed. Reg. 21226, Apr. 23, 2010, available at http://ntia.doc.gov/frnotices/2010/FR_PrivacyNOI_04232010.pdf.

[112]In 2003, FTC began implementing the National Do Not Call Registry, which allows consumers to register to prevent unwanted telemarketing calls. The registry was the result of FTC's Telemarketing Sales Rule, which implemented the Telemarketing and Consumer Fraud and Abuse Prevention Act of 1994, and the Federal Communication Commission's rules and regulations implementing the Telephone Consumer Protection Act of 1991.

[113]Department of Commerce, Internet Policy Task Force, *Commercial Data Privacy and Innovation in the Internet Economy: A Dynamic Policy Framework* (Washington, D.C.: 2010).

to track and comply with data protection laws in each country. Specifically, some who commented noted gaps in protection for consumers whose data were transferred across borders, because it was not always clear who had jurisdiction over data and what protections existed for foreign consumers. To overcome these obstacles, they recommended a number of options, with the majority advocating for greater harmonization and the ability to work together across systems (interoperability).[114] The Administration's 2012 privacy framework echoed these concerns and noted that creating interoperability between different nations' privacy regimes was critical to the continued growth of the digital economy. Underlying the approach to achieving international interoperability, it said, were mutual recognition of commercial data privacy frameworks, cooperation in enforcing these frameworks, and mechanisms that allow companies to demonstrate accountability.

As noted previously, the European Union's 1995 Data Protection Directive provides a comprehensive privacy framework and states that the personal information of European Union citizens may not be transmitted to nations not deemed to have "adequate" data protection laws. The United States does not have an adequacy finding from the European Commission (the executive body of the European Union). However, companies that participate in the U.S.-EU Safe Harbor Framework are deemed to provide adequate data protections and may transfer personal data from the European Union.[115] Some industry observers have warned against enacting a strict privacy regime like the one in the European Union. For example, according to a representative of an information reseller, moving to a strict privacy regime similar to that of the European Union would hinder commerce and innovation and have a strongly detrimental effect on certain industries and the overall U.S. economy. A representative of another information reseller said that the U.S. privacy regime has worked well and agreed that making it more like that of the European Union would have detrimental, unintended consequences, such as harming economic growth and innovation.

---

[114]Such measures would augment existing frameworks for interoperability of data. For example, the July 2000 U.S.-EU Safe Harbor intergovernmental agreement facilitates interoperability between the privacy regimes in the United States and the European Union. The framework provides a method for U.S. companies to transfer personal data outside the European Union in a way that is consistent with EU data protection laws.

[115]FTC has the authority to enforce the substantive privacy requirements of the U.S.-EU Safe Harbor Framework.

Conclusions

The advent of new and more advanced technologies and changes in the marketplace for consumer information have vastly increased the amount and nature of personal information collected and the number of parties that use or share this information. While the views of stakeholders differ, based on our review, we found that gaps exist in the current statutory privacy framework. In particular, the current framework does not fully address changes in technology and marketplace practices that fundamentally have altered the nature and extent to which personal information is being shared with third parties. Moreover, while current laws protect privacy interests in specific sectors and for specific uses, consumers have little control over how their information is collected, used, and shared with third parties for marketing purposes. As a result, current privacy law is not always aligned with the Fair Information Practice Principles, which Commerce and others have said should serve as the foundation for commercial data privacy.

Thus, the current privacy framework warrants reconsideration in relation to a number of issues, including consumers' ability to access, correct, and control their personal information used for marketing; the types of personal information collected and the sources and methods for collecting it; and privacy controls related to relatively new technologies, such as web tracking and mobile devices. At the same time, different legislative approaches to improving privacy—including comprehensive or sector-specific—involve trade-offs and have advantages and disadvantages. The challenge will be providing appropriate privacy protections without unduly inhibiting the benefits to consumers, commerce, and innovation that data sharing can accord.

Matter for Congressional Consideration

Congress should consider strengthening the current consumer privacy framework to reflect the effects of changes in technology and the marketplace—particularly in relation to consumer data used for marketing purposes—while also ensuring that any limitations on data collection and sharing do not unduly inhibit the economic and other benefits to industry and consumers that data sharing can accord. Among the issues that should be considered are

- the adequacy of consumers' ability to access, correct, and control their personal information in circumstances beyond those currently accorded under FCRA;
- whether there should be additional controls on the types of personal or sensitive information that may or may not be collected and shared;

- changes needed, if any, in the permitted sources and methods for data collection; and
- privacy controls related to new technologies, such as web tracking and mobile devices.

Agency Comments

We provided a draft of this report for review and comment to the Department of Commerce and the Federal Trade Commission. In written comments, which are reprinted in appendix III, Commerce agreed that evolving technology and business practices are changing the ways that consumers' personal information is collected and used, and that strengthened privacy protections could better protect consumers and support innovation. It also noted that the Administration's privacy framework supports privacy legislation that would create baseline protections for consumers while preserving existing sector-specific federal laws. In addition, the Federal Trade Commission provided technical comments, which we incorporated as appropriate.

As agreed with your office, unless you publicly announce its contents earlier, we plan no further distribution of this report until 30 days from the report date. At that time, we will provide copies to other interested congressional committees, as well as the Secretary of Commerce and the Chairman of the Federal Trade Commission. We will also make copies available to others upon request. In addition, this report will be available at no charge on our website at http://www.gao.gov.

Should you or your staff have questions concerning this report, please contact me at (202) 512-8678 or cackleya@gao.gov. Contact points for our Offices of Congressional Relations and Public Affairs may be found on the last page of this report. Key contributors to this report are listed in appendix IV.

Sincerely yours,

Alicia Puente Cackley
Director
Financial Markets and
    Community Investment

Appendix I: Objectives, Scope, and Methodology

This report examines (1) existing federal laws relating to the privacy of consumer information held by information resellers, (2) any gaps that may exist in this legal framework, and (3) views on approaches for improving consumer data privacy. For the purposes of this report, we defined information resellers as companies with a primary line of business of collecting, aggregating, and selling publicly available and private personal information to third parties. This report focuses primarily on privacy issues related to consumer information used for marketing and for individual reference services—sometimes called look-up or people-search services. We generally excluded from our review privacy issues related to consumer data collected and used by information resellers for purposes such as fraud prevention, eligibility determination for credit or employment, and legal compliance.

To determine laws that relate to the privacy and safeguarding of consumer information held by information resellers, we reviewed relevant federal and selected state laws and determined their applicability to information resellers' collection and use of consumer information used for marketing and individual reference services. Specifically, we reviewed various law review and legal journal articles, conducted searches of the Westlaw database, and reviewed and analyzed a legal treatise compiling laws relating to data privacy, including any laws applicable to government records, electronic surveillance, medical data, financial information, commercial transactions, and online activity.[1] We reviewed laws in terms of their general purpose, applicability to resellers or the collection and use of consumer information, as well as applicable agency regulations.

In conducting our analyses, we determined that privacy laws are applicable for specific purposes, in certain situations, to certain sectors, to certain types of entities, or to certain types of records; and categorized our findings into two major groups that included (1) primary federal privacy laws, and (2) other federal privacy laws that also may apply to information resellers' practices and products, consumer services, or types of records. We also reviewed and analyzed relevant state laws governing consumer privacy and data security, and identified those states that also enacted privacy legislation beyond data breach notification. We reviewed selected Federal Trade Commission (FTC) enforcement actions related to its deception and unfairness authority. To determine whether gaps may

---

[1]D. Reed Freeman and J. Trevor Hughes, *Privacy Law in Marketing* (2013).

exist in the current privacy framework, we analyzed these federal laws
and related regulations to assess the extent of privacy protections under
federal law and any limitations in their scope, including the adequacy of
consumers' ability to access, correct, opt out, or request deletion of
information.

To obtain views on approaches to improving consumer data privacy—as
well as gather additional information on potential gaps in the privacy
framework for consumer privacy—we identified and analyzed relevant
studies and reports, Congressional testimony, legislative and regulatory
proposals, position papers, and other documents from governmental and
nongovernmental stakeholders. We solicited views on these issues from
representatives of various organizations that represent the interests of
information resellers, advertisers, and consumers, as well as federal
agencies. We reviewed the Fair Information Practice Principles (FIPPs), a
set of internationally recognized principles for protecting the privacy and
security of personal information, and the framework for consumer data
privacy issued by the White House in February 2012. We also reviewed
relevant public comments that the Department of Commerce (Commerce)
and FTC received from notices soliciting such comments. In addition, we
reviewed correspondence from information resellers in response to the
Bipartisan Congressional Privacy Caucus's inquiry into nine resellers' use
of consumer information.[2]

To address all three objectives, we also used Internet search techniques
and keyword search terms to identify sources and types of available
information about the reseller industry, including the definition of
information resellers; number and nature of companies that serve as
information resellers; industry revenues; product offerings; internal
controls and practices; extent of consumer information collected and
maintained; and who is buying information resellers' products and for
what purposes. In doing so, we generally obtained information from
various online research sources such as LexisNexis, Proquest, and
Gartner, which consisted of company dossiers, journals, trade
publications, periodicals, studies, white papers, and aggregated
databases relevant to the reseller industry. We also analyzed U.S.

---

[2]On July 25, 2012, the Bipartisan Congressional Privacy Caucus sent letters to
information resellers requesting data about the collection and use of consumers' personal
information. The nine resellers that responded to the congressional inquiry were Acxiom,
Epsilon, Equifax, Experian, FICO, Harte-Hanks, Intelius, Merkle, and Meredith.

Census Bureau data to obtain information on business classification
codes (including Standard Industrial Classification and North American
Classification System codes) assigned to reseller companies to classify
their main industry and line of business. On the basis of our analyses, we
determined that the data do not provide a reliable count or other statistical
information on the information reseller industry, and there is limited
publicly known information about the industry as a whole.

We obtained documentation from, and interviewed representatives of,
federal agencies, including the Consumer Financial Protection Bureau,
Commerce, and FTC; trade associations, including the Consumer Data
Industry Association and Direct Marketing Association; consumer and
privacy advocacy organizations, including the Center for Digital
Democracy, Electronic Privacy Information Center, Privacy Rights
Clearinghouse, U.S. Public Interest Research Group, and World Privacy
Forum; Privacy Times, a newsletter that covers privacy law and policy;
and Safe Shepherd, a company that provides products and services to
protect privacy. In addition, we interviewed (in some cases, receiving
written responses to questions we provided) six information resellers—
Acxiom, Epsilon, Experian Marketing, Intelius, LexisNexis (Reed
Elsevier), and Spokeo. These companies were selected because, based
on our analyses, they constituted a mix of the largest and most widely
recognized resellers that maintain a range of products and services that
collect and sell consumer information for purposes including marketing,
individual reference services, or both. The information resellers we
included and the products they offer do not necessarily represent the full
scope of the industry. We reviewed marketing materials and other
documentation from these companies. Additionally, we reviewed our 2006
and 2008 reports on information resellers as well as recent work on
issues related to consumer and data privacy, and other related subjects.[3]

We conducted this performance audit from August 2012 through
September 2013, in accordance with generally accepted government
auditing standards. Those standards require that we plan and perform the

---

[3]See GAO, *Personal Information: Agency and Reseller Adherence to Key Privacy
Principles*, GAO-06-421 (Washington, D.C.: Apr. 4, 2006). *Personal Information: Key
Federal Privacy Laws Do Not Require Information Resellers to Safeguard All Sensitive
Data*, GAO-06-674 (Washington, D.C.: June 26, 2006); and *Privacy: Government Use of
Data from Information Resellers Could Include Better Protections*, GAO-08-543T
(Washington, D.C.: Mar. 11, 2008).

audit to obtain sufficient, appropriate evidence to provide a reasonable basis for our findings and conclusions based on our audit objectives. We believe that the evidence obtained provides a reasonable basis for our findings and conclusions based on our audit objectives.

Appendix II: Examples of Data Collected and Used by Information Resellers

Tables 2 and 3 illustrate some of the consumer information included in the marketing products offered by two large information resellers, Acxiom and Experian Marketing.

Table 2: Selected Examples of Consumer Data in Acxiom's Marketing Products, 2012

Category	Selected Elements
Individual data	Name, address, telephone number, e-mail, gender, education, occupation, voter party, ethnic code/language preference, age, date of birth.
Household demographics	Adult age ranges, children's age ranges, gender, number of adults and number of children in the household, marital status.
Household purchase behavior	Frequency of purchase indicator, types of purchases indicator, charitable giving indicator, community involvement indicator, average direct mail purchase amount, direct mail frequency indicator.
Household life event indicators	New parent, expectant parents, new teen driver, college graduate, empty nester, new mover, recent home buyer, recent mortgage borrower, getting married, divorced, child leaving home, buying a new car.
Household wealth indicators	Estimated household income ranges, income producing assets indicator, estimated net worth ranges.
Household vehicle data	Year, make, model, estimated vehicle value, vehicle lifestyle indicator, model and brand affinity, used vehicle preference indicator.
Household social media predictors	Social media sites l kely to be used by an individual or household, heavy or light user, whether they engage in public social media activities such as signing on to fan pages or posting or viewing YouTube videos.

Source: Acxiom.

Note: According to Acxiom, detailed transaction-level data, Social Security numbers, driver's license numbers, and known instances of personally identifiable information about children under age 18 are excluded from these marketing products.

Table 3: Selected Examples of Marketing Lists Available from Experian, 2012

Category	Marketing Lists
Hobbies and interests	Astrology/psychic reading, boating, gardening, photography, politics, religion, self-improvement, volunteering.
Pet owners	Cats, dogs, other pets.
Reading preferences	Bible/devotional, children's, history, mystery, nonfiction, romance, science fiction.
Collecting	Art/antiques, die cast miniatures, dolls, plates, sports memorabilia, stamps/coins.
Cooking and entertaining	Baking, gourmet cooking, recipes, wine appreciation.
Health and fitness	Healthy living, interest in fitness, natural/herbal remedies, personal care/beauty care, reduce fat/cholesterol, vegetarian, weight conscious.
Music preference	Christian, classical/opera/big band, country, jazz/new age, oldies, rhythm and blues, rock
Sweepstakes and gambling	Casino gambling, lotteries, sweepstakes.
Sports and recreation	Boating/sailing, camping/hiking, fishing, golf, hunting, motorcycles, racing/autos, running/jogging, skiing, swimming, tennis, outdoors.
Occupation	Beauty (cosmetologists, barbers, manicurists) civil servants, clergy, clerical/office workers, doctors/physicians/surgeons, executives/administrators, farming/agriculture, health services, middle management, nurses, professional/technical, retail service, retired, sales, marketing, self-employed, skilled/trade/machine operator/laborer, teacher/educator.
Financial investments	Certificates of deposit/money market funds, mutual funds/annuities, Individual Retirement Accounts, life insurance, real estate, stocks or bonds.
Ailments	Allergies, Alzheimer's disease, angina, arthritis/rheumatism, asthma, back pain, cancer, clinical depression, diabetes, emphysema, erectile dysfunction, epilepsy, frequent heartburn, gum problems, hearing difficulty, high blood pressure, high cholesterol, irritable bowel syndrome, lactose intolerant, ulcer, menopause, migraines/frequent headaches, multiple sclerosis, osteoporosis, Parkinson's disease, prostate problems, psoriasis/eczema, sinusitis/sinuses.
Visual impairments	Contact lenses, eyeglasses, visual impairments/correction.

Source: Experian Marketing Services.

Note: According to Experian Marketing Services, its marketing lists derive primarily from (1) self-reported survey data provided directly by the consumer with consent; (2) purchase categories provided by retailers after the retailer has provided its customer a notice and ability to opt-out of such information sharing; and (3) public records. Marketing lists are not composed of fewer than 50 addresses and Experian policy and user agreements allow recipients of the lists to use them only for direct marketing purposes.

Appendix III: Comments from the Department of Commerce

THE DEPUTY SECRETARY OF COMMERCE
Washington, D.C. 20230

September 10, 2013

The Honorable Gene L. Dodaro
Comptroller General of the United States
U.S. Government Accountability Office
441 G Street NW
Washington, DC 20548-0002

Dear Mr. Dodaro:

Thank you for the opportunity to comment on the Government Accountability Office (GAO) draft report entitled, "Information Resellers: Consumer Privacy Framework Needs to Reflect Changes in Technology and the Marketplace," GAO 13-663. I appreciate the work the GAO has done to analyze information resellers' business practices and the applicable legal regime, as well as the consumer privacy issues raised by these practices.

I agree that evolving technology and business practices are changing the ways that consumers' personal information is collected and used. I also agree that strengthened privacy protections could better protect consumers and support innovation.

The Obama Administration's Privacy Blueprint[1] supports privacy legislation that would create baseline protections for consumers while preserving existing sector-specific Federal laws. As your report observes, such baseline legislation would provide protections for the portions of the information reseller market not currently covered by Federal privacy laws. The Privacy Blueprint also calls for stakeholder-developed codes of conduct to complement statutory privacy safeguards.

The National Telecommunications and Information Administration (NTIA) is working to implement the Privacy Blueprint by convening stakeholder groups tasked with developing codes of conduct that apply widely accepted privacy principles to specific business sectors. Codes of conduct can provide consumers with access to, and greater control over, their personal information.

---

[1] The Executive Office of the President, *Consumer Data Privacy in a Networked World: A Framework for Protecting Privacy and Promoting Innovation in the Global Digital Economy*, Feb. 23, 2012, available at http://www.whitehouse.gov/sites/default/files/privacy-final.pdf (Blueprint).

The Honorable Gene L. Dodaro
Page 2

Thank you again for the opportunity to review and comment on the draft report.

Sincerely,

Patrick Gallagher
Acting Deputy Secretary of
Commerce

Appendix IV: GAO Contact and Staff Acknowledgments

GAO Contact	Alicia Puente Cackley, 202-512-8678 or cackleya@gao.gov
Staff Acknowledgments	In addition to the contact named above, Jason Bromberg (Assistant Director), Michelle Bowsky, William R. Chatlos, Rachel DeMarcus, Beth Faraguna, Kun-Fang Lee, Patricia Moye, Barbara Roesmann, Rachel Siegel, and Jena Sinkfield made key contributions to this report.